A MOTHER'S BOOK OF WIT & WISDOM

CHERI FULLER

Enjoy this season of mothering!
— Cheri Fuller

NAVPRESS ◢

BRINGING TRUTH TO LIFE

NavPress Publishing Group

P.O. Box 35001, Colorado Springs, Colorado 80935

The Navigators is an international Christian organization. Jesus Christ gave His followers the Great Commission to go and make disciples (Matthew 28:19). The aim of The Navigators is to help fulfill that commission by multiplying laborers for Christ in every nation.

NavPress is the publishing ministry of The Navigators. NavPress publications are tools to help Christians grow. Although publications alone cannot make disciples or change lives, they can help believers learn biblical discipleship, and apply what they learn to their lives and ministries.

Some of the anecdotal illustrations in this book are true to life and are included with the permission of the persons involved. All other illustrations are composites of real situations, and any resemblance to people living or dead is coincidental.

Scripture quotations in this publication are taken from the *New American Standard Bible* (NASB), © The Lockman Foundation 1960, 1962, 1963, 1968, 1971, 1972, 1973, 1975, 1977; the *HOLY BIBLE: NEW INTERNATIONAL VERSION®* (NIV®), Copyright © 1973, 1978, 1984 by International Bible Society, used by permission of Zondervan Publishing House, all rights reserved; *The Living Bible* (TLB), © 1971 owned by assignment by the Illinois Regional Bank N.A. (as trustee), used by permission of Tyndale House Publishers, Inc., Wheaton, IL 60189; and *The Message: New Testament with Psalms and Proverbs* by Eugene H. Peterson, copyright © 1993, 1995, used by permission of NavPress Publishing Group.

1 2 3 4 5 6 7 8 9 10 11 12 13 14 15 16 17 18 19 20 / 99 98 97 96 95

Printed in the United States of America

—————————
Published in association
with the literary agency of
Alive Communications, P.O. Box 49068,
Colorado Springs, CO 80949.
—————————

FOR A FREE CATALOG OF
NAVPRESS BOOKS & BIBLE STUDIES,
CALL 1-800-366-7788 (USA)
or 1-416-499-4615 (CANADA)
—————————

*This book is dedicated to my mother-in-law, Joan Fuller,
who has been a wonderful mother to me and grandmother to our
children. And along with Joan, to those women who provided
a mother's nurturing, encouragement, love, and godly role models in
my life since my mom joined my dad in Heaven in 1982: Billie Milburn,
Patty Johnston, and Flo Perkins. To them and to all those heroines
of the faith, women writers and mothers who have recorded their
insights and wisdom and from whom I have gained immensely as
a wife and mother, I am deeply grateful. You have blazed the trail. You
have kept the faith, and there is a crown awaiting you!*

*"Since we have such a huge crowd of men [and women] of faith
watching us from the grandstands, let us strip off anything that slows
us down or holds us back, and especially those sins that wrap
themselves so tightly around our feet and trip us up; and let us run
with patience the particular race that God has set before us.
Keep your eyes on Jesus, our leader and instructor."*

Hebrews 12:1-2 (TLB)

AUTHOR

Cheri Fuller is an experienced educator and has taught every level from elementary to college. She is the author of several previous books and numerous articles in *Family Circle, Child, Parents of Teenagers, Focus on the Family*, and others. She has also appeared on numerous television and radio programs, and is a popular speaker to conferences, parent groups, and teacher seminars. She and her husband, Holmes, live in Oklahoma City with their three children.

A NOTE TO MOMS

Most of us mothers are extremely busy—parenting, making a home for our families, cooking, carpooling, and some juggling an in-home business or out-of-the-home job. Many of you are also homeschooling your children, and lots of others volunteer at your kids' schools. Perhaps like me, on many days you find yourself short of time but you want to be the best mom you can be. That's where this book will come in handy—by giving daily nuggets of wisdom and encouragement on the subject that is close to our hearts—being a mother.

Besides my own insights and what I've learned in the process of mothering Justin (who as of this year is twenty-three, out of college, and married), Christopher, twenty, a college student, and Alison, eighteen, who is on the verge of high school graduation, you'll also find counsel and wisdom from some of my favorite Christian mothers and grandmothers. From women as diverse as Anne Bradstreet, an American colonial mother and writer, to my own mother, and women I greatly admire like Edith Schaeffer, Madeleine L'Engle, and Marjorie Holmes, all have gone before us and offer both wisdom and wit for the journey. Some special mothers across the country also contributed their insights on childrearing.

In the pages ahead you'll find 365 inspiring quotes or sayings on motherhood, prayer, meeting children's and teens' needs, building security at home, celebrating life, strengthening marriage, your own spiritual growth, and many other topics. After the thought or quote is a practical way to apply it or a how-to tip on the subject. There's also humor to lighten your load, and pithy sayings by some wise men. (We wouldn't want to leave them out!)

Many of these sayings and insights have been on my bulletin board or refrigerator and have proven to be of particular help to me in parenting my own three children through their growing-up years.

Mothering is a learning process, and we grow as our children grow—day by day. When we hold our little one right after delivery, we don't have all the insight, knowhow, or patience we'll need. It's a process of learning, becoming, of enlarging our hearts, growing in our relationships with our families, and most of all, with the Lord—for He is the One who gives us the strength, love, and perseverance we need for each day. I hope this book will give you much encouragement and many practical ideas for creative mothering and raising kids with strong values and purpose.

Regardless of the age of your child, I hope in these pages you will gain a bigger picture of the mothering journey. If you have small children and you find a quote or tip on parenting teenagers, enjoy it and tuck the idea away for a day that's not too far away. Adolescence will be here before you know it! Keep a spiral notebook or journal handy for the "nuggets" that ask you to reflect on a question or to list things as you think of them (gifts and talents of each child, or blessings you've received, for example).

Unattributed quotes bearing the symbol ⌒ are my own; others followed by the symbol ⬤ are from anonymous authors or unknown sources. If you'd like to read more from a particular author, refer to the bibliography at the end of the book for a listing of all the resources.

1

*The chain of a mother's prayers
can link her child to God.*

Pray for each of your children while you engage
in a daily chore or activity—for your oldest child
while you set the table for breakfast, for your youngest
while you cook dinner, for your middle child
while you do laundry.

2

*We all have a story to tell—a treasure chest to open
for our children. Each person has a rich storehouse of tales:
stories of broken bones and first dates, sorrows and joys,
overcoming adversities and trusting God.*

Use trips and errand time in the car to tell
your child stories of your own childhood:
▶ your first stitches or black eye;
▶ mischief and misadventures you got into;
▶ when you first accepted Christ into your life;
▶ your first camp experience or the first
Christmas you remember.

3

Time goes by so quickly,
and there's so much to teach our children!
ERMA BOMBECK

Watch for "teachable moments,"
those natural opportunities for talking with your child
about your values, knowledge, and ideas;
moments for encouraging his natural curiosity
by answering his questions
about why clouds form
and lightning strikes.

4

Words have the power to boost or deflate
a child's self-worth, to hurt or inspire him,
to cheer or to discourage him.
Choose your words wisely!

Instead of saying "Why can't you be like
your brother?" try substituting encouraging words
such as "You are really improving," "I know you can
do it," "Now, that's a great idea!" and best of all,
"I love you, and God loves you even more."

5

*Every day is a gift from God,
so there is always something to celebrate—
a colorful sunset, a rainbow, the first snowfall.*

One of the best ways to celebrate and make
your family feel cared for is to decorate your dining
table: Put a pot of flowers or a basket of shells
in the center of the table. Try different things
for different seasons: flags for July 4th, green apples
and candles or pinecones on a fall day.

6

*When ordinary mothers pray,
extraordinary things happen.*

Personalize your prayers by putting your child's name
in a Scripture passage that communicates your hopes
and desires for her. For example: "I pray that the eyes
of [Jamie's] heart will be opened so that she may *know*
the hope of Christ's calling and what is the incredible
greatness of His power toward those who believe"
(see Ephesians 1:18).

7

There is a love that never ends
between the hearts of special friends.

Is there another mother you can call today
to encourage, empathize, talk, or pray with?
Perhaps you could invite her over for a cup of tea.

8

Babies are angels whose wings grow shorter
as their legs grow longer.

You and your child could have a teddy bear
tea party or a picnic at a nearby lake or pond.
Or just serve a silly meal. Enjoy your child's
growing up years—they speed by so quickly!

9

What a mother should save
for a rainy day is patience.

On a rainy or cold day, when "cabin fever" has set in,
give your child an old sheet to drape over a table,
a few small pillows, some favorite books, and a snack
in his lunch box. With this "rainy-day hideaway"
the day will be much more pleasant.

10

One of a child's deepest needs is to be appreciated.
As many times as you correct your child,
be sure to balance it with praise.
FERN NICHOLS

11

Prayer should be the key of the day
and the lock of the night.

Begin and end your child's day with prayer.
Times of illness, problems at school, or frustrations
with friends—in all these situations you can help
your child turn to God so that she will sense
His presence in all of life.

12

We never appreciate the love of our mothers for us
until we become mothers.

Write *your* mother a thank-you letter for her character
qualities, for all the cookies she baked, PTA meetings
she attended, birthday parties she threw, and zany
memories from your growing-up years.

13

With eight of my eleven grandchildren now owning
driver's licenses, I am glad that Corrie ten Boom gave me
the Lord's private telephone number—JE 333, for Jeremiah
33:3—and it's available to His children twenty-four hours of
every day. You just have to "call to Him, and He will answer
you and He will tell you great and mighty things,
which you do not know."
DOROTHY SHELLENBERGER

Dial the Lord's private telephone number today when
you have concerns about your child—when you need
wisdom for the challenges and duties you face.

14

Always remember to forget
The troubles that passed away.
But never forget to remember
The blessings that come each day.

Make a basketful of gratefulness for your table.
Put slips of paper in it for family members
to write about things, people, or activities
they are thankful for.
Read the blessings on Sundays at mealtime.

15

Being a mom is like a circle. Because we are surrounded by constant challenges and changes that seem to pull us apart at times, we need to have an inside that stays intact.
DORIS DIENER, FROM AN INTERVIEW

Keep your "inside" intact by having a quiet time each day. No matter how busy you are, you can still meditate on a Scripture verse while you do dishes or read a psalm and talk to God about your day.

16

Lord, help our marriage, and let it begin with me.
ELISABETH ALEXANDER

When you have a problem or conflict with your husband, pray this prayer and be open to God bringing change first in *you*.

17

Fear not for tomorrow;
God is already there.

Write down your fears or anxieties and give them to God one by one. Trust Him with them, thank and praise Him, and then determine *not* to fret about them.

18

*Once when my children were young,
I heard a mother screaming at her children, and I thought,
"She wouldn't treat someone outside the family or a stranger
like that. How sad that she would speak to her own children
that way." I purposed, then and there, to speak with love
and respect to my children, even when correcting them.*

JOAN FULLER,
FROM AN INTERVIEW

▶ Avoid name-calling, sarcasm, and screaming.
Instead act and react in love.
▶ Encourage your children to speak to each other
in as kind and friendly a voice
as they would their friends.

19

*Children are strongly influenced by a parent's
expectations and will live up or down to what you believe
they will do. If they hear positive expectations,
then they do much better in the classroom.*

DR. CAROL KELLY,
FROM AN INTERVIEW

Instead of using negative labels, which express
low expectations for your child, communicate high
expectations: "You'll do fine in math; think of all the
times you've helped me measure when we cook
and when we add up items at the grocery store"
or "You've been so organized about your homework!
I think I'll put you in charge of the family calendar."

20

Everywhere, we learn from those we love.
GOETHE

Notice all the things you can learn from your children,
especially things about God like:
- ▶ Kids tend to pray with an assurance of answers that
adults lack. You can learn faith from your child.
- ▶ Children are down to earth about prayer: They pray
about practical stuff like their baseball games
and their pets, all of which God cares about.

21

*Childhood is that wonderful time when all you need
to do to lose weight is bathe.*

Cut out bright-colored sponges in animal shapes
for your child to play with in the bathtub. Add some
mild shaving cream to do "art" on the tub.
And don't forget the giggles!

22

Family faces are magic mirrors. Looking at people who belong to us, we see the past, present, and future. We make discoveries about ourselves.
GAIL LUMET BUCKLEY,
THE HORNES: AN AMERICAN FAMILY

Make a photo album for your child to keep in her room—pictures of great-grandparents, grandparents, special relatives, cousins, parents, and siblings. Let her write captions below each picture describing the memory represented or something unique about the person.

23

As we encourage our children, they grow in confidence and become encouragers themselves. Someday, when you need it the most and least expect it, your son or daughter will come alongside and say just the right building-up words you need to keep going or to face a trial.

Encourage your child with a smile and a hug as he returns home. Say positive, encouraging words today and every day.

24

*A mother should be like a quilt—keeping her children warm
but not smothering them.*

Help your children develop relationships with
each other and with friends by having special times
to play and talk when you are occupied
in another part of the house.

25

*I have found that my confidence in being a godly mother
springs from a deepening relationship with the Lord
rather than from measuring how I am doing by looking at
my children's behavior. My consistent walk with God enables
me to be sensitive to the Lord's wisdom and direction in loving
and training my children, and it enables God to free me from
wanting to control them so that I will look good.*
CYNTHIA HEALD

What do you put your confidence in today—
your children's behavior or your relationship with God
and His faithfulness? Ask for a closer, more consistent
walk with Him and the freedom from trying
to control your kids.

26

The future is as bright as the promises of God.

Each week, write on a large index card a promise
of God, such as, "For I know the plans I have for you,
says the Lord. They are plans for good and not for evil,
to give you a future and a hope" (Jeremiah 29:11, TLB).
Let your child illustrate the promise or draw a symbol
to remember it by, and post the card
on the refrigerator.

27

You may have tangible wealth untold
Caskets of jewels and coffers of gold.
Richer than I you can never be—
I had a mother who read to me.
STRICKLAND GILLILAN,
"THE READING MOTHER"

Keep a basket of books by your child's bed
and save twenty to thirty minutes at bedtime
to read her stories of fanciful flights of imagination,
Bible stories, and poetry.

28

It will be gone before you know it.
The fingerprints on the wall appear higher and higher.
Then suddenly they disappear.
DOROTHY EVSLIN

Put several different colors of bright acrylic paint in
pie pans, have your children carefully stick their left
hands in one color to make a handprint on the front
of a white adult-sized T-shirt. Have them do the same
with their right hands, using another color. Under
each set of handprints, have each child write his name
with a paintbrush. Let it dry and you have a wonderful
T-shirt personalized by your favorite hands.

29

What the mother sings to the cradle
goes all the way down to the coffin.
HENRY WARD BEECHER,
PROVERBS FROM PLYMOUTH PULPIT

Sing to your child as you care for her
and go about your day; sing praise choruses,
favorite songs, and little verses set to music about her:
"You are my joy! You look so sweet today!"
When you ride in the car together, sing happy songs
and when you put her to bed, sing soothing hymns,
folk songs, and lullabies.

30

*For those mothers concerned about their children
in the public schools, I would say: What a wonderful
opportunity to trust God to keep that which we've committed
to Him, and to teach our children that God's grace
keeps pace with whatever we face.*

DOROTHY BURSHEK,
FROM AN INTERVIEW

If your children are in public school:
- ▶ Pray with them daily.
- ▶ Have open communication about
  what they are learning.
- ▶ Read Scripture about problems they are facing.
- ▶ Join a Moms-in-Touch group to pray weekly with
other mothers for the school, the teachers, your child,
and classmates. Call 1-800-949-MOMS.

31

*A baby is a kiss from heaven
blown from the hand of God.*

Take many photographs of your children—
especially of them sleeping. Keep a small album
of these photos in your purse to pull out
and remind you of those special peaceful moments.

32

*Mothering is the art of bringing children up
without putting them down.*

What are you grateful for about your child?
Write a list and keep it in your Bible or journal.
Thank God for these strengths, especially during
the prickly or difficult stages she goes through.
Whenever the opportunity arises, say something
to her about her progress or gifts in these areas.

33

*Throughout the ages, no country has had a better friend
than the mother who taught her children to pray.*

After your evening meal, have prayer as a family. Talk
about what each child's needs are—tests at school,
peer pressure, family members or friends he or she is
concerned for. Then divvy up the needs and let
everyone pray for different things. Be sure to thank
God for His blessings and for your family.

34

*Say only what is good and helpful to those you are talking to,
and what will give them a blessing.*
EPHESIANS 4:29 (TLB)

Focus on the donut instead of the hole—
the eighty-five points your teen got right
on the math test instead of the fifteen he missed;
the good sportsmanship and effort he displayed
in the soccer game instead of the goal he missed.
In doing this, you'll be giving him a blessing.

35

*Reading consists mainly of thinking; only a small part
consists of the reader's eyes moving across the page. If
children are going to become good readers, they need many
opportunities to dialogue and practice critical thinking.*

Help your child think critically by having him tell you
the most significant idea he got out of a book he read
for school or out of a course or activity. Ask questions
like "What is your understanding of this situation?"
or "What are some solutions for this problem?"

36

Only if a teenager's emotional tank is full
can he be expected to be his best and do his best.
DR. ROSS CAMPBELL,
HOW TO REALLY LOVE YOUR TEENAGER

Fill your young person's emotional tank by giving focused attention. Full, undivided attention, even for a few moments a day, can help him feel truly loved and worth your time, caring, and appreciation.

37

You can support your adolescent's growing independence
by encouraging small steps toward autonomy, gradually
transferring responsibility so that he is weaned away from
your control and develops the skills to succeed
by the time he leaves home.

Gradually increase your teen's responsibilities and privileges. For example, if in the ninth grade his curfew was 11:00 p.m. on weekends, it might become 12:00 p.m. in his junior year, 12:30 p.m. during senior year first semester, and then lifted in the last semester before graduation, as long as he communicates with you about his schedule. Then, by the first year of college, he has been responsible and has practiced handling the "no curfew" policy of most dormitories and tends not to go wild with the newfound freedom.

38

*Worry is like a rocking chair; it gives you something to do,
but it won't get you anywhere.*

Remember that a large part of what we worry about
doesn't come true—the lesser part happens and we
can't control it anyway! Jot down your worries
one by one, pray, and release them to God.
Determine not to worry today.

39

*Authority without wisdom is like a heavy axe
without an edge, fitter to bruise than polish.*
**ANNE BRADSTREET,
"MEDITATIONS DIVINE AND MORAL"**

Seek for more wisdom in mothering your children:
▸ Study a biblical proverb a day;
they are full of wisdom for parenting.
▸ Attend a parenting seminar
or mothers' support group.
▸ Listen to a book on tape or read a book on
individual differences in children
(see bibliography at end of book).

40

Everybody makes mistakes.
That's why pencils have erasers!

Help your young person put his mistakes in
perspective and realize that they are wonderful
opportunities to learn. Tell him about some of your
biggest "teen blunders"—your first fender-bender,
worst date, or a significant decision.

41

The Christian is not one who has gone all the way
with Christ. None of us has. The Christian is one who
has found the right road.
CHARLES L. ALLEN

Find biographies and magazine profiles
of men and women who have
"found the right road" and are making an impact
for Christ in the world around them.
Share what you find with your child.

42

I'm surrounded by parents who have their kids in every possible after-school activity. When I start getting caught up in the craziness, I stop and ask myself, "What kind of person would I really like my child to be? Do I want a Type A character who is fantastically successful but always feels tremendous pressure to perform?"
ANNE PRESCOTT

What kind of person would you like your child to be? Does your family's lifestyle support that development? What changes could you make—
limiting extracurricular activities to provide time for play? Finding a balance between family and job/school responsibilities? Nurturing spiritual values?

43

Time to talk and a mom to listen are the best medicine for many of the fears, disappointments, and struggles of adolescence.

Make time on a regular basis after your teen gets home from school or right before bedtime just to listen to her and perhaps ask a few nonintrusive questions such as, "I'd like to hear about your day—what was the highlight and the low point today?" or "Can you give me a word picture of how you've been feeling about things today?"

44

Families who practice traditions and rituals are 37 percent less likely than other families to have delinquent, chemically dependent, or underachieving teens.
H. Stephen Glenn, *Raising Self-Reliant Children in a Self-Indulgent World*

Don't give up your family traditions when your kids reach adolescence. Instead, have a family discussion about Christmas and other holidays. Start with questions such as: What have you enjoyed *most* (and least) that we've done in the past? What holiday activities, if discontinued, would make it not seem like Christmas to you? What is one thing you would like to change in next year's celebration? Apply their answers to other holidays and events; adjust traditions, but continue them throughout the growing-up years.

45

Happy is the mom who is too busy to worry in the daytime and too sleepy to worry at night.

Ask yourself: Can God and I handle what's going on right now? Forget the "what ifs"—we *can't* handle them! Instead, thank Him that He's working for your good in any situation.

46

*We can't put our teens in a protective bubble until
they get through adolescence. We can't be in the car with
them after every football game or party. But God has given
us a powerful resource in prayer and we can be on our
knees regularly on their behalf.*

Meet with another mother who has teenagers
and also has a desire to pray for them. Pray together
at least an hour a week for your children, their friends,
and their schools.

47

There is no such thing as a nonworking mother!

If your work is an in-home business or out-of-the-
home job, take a day to show your teen what you do;
take her to a "working lunch" and talk about some
of the challenges you face and show her products
or other results of what you do.

48

When you get to your wit's end,
you'll find God lives there.
ELIZABETH YATES,
A BOOK OF HOURS

When you are stressed by the demands of parenting
a child or teenager, take a break with God. Find a
quiet place, take out some paper, and list your
struggles, needs, and hopes regarding your child.
Read something inspirational, breathe deeply,
and take a walk around the block.

49

My mother came to all my performances. She'd lead the
laughter and applause. If anybody spoke too loudly or
coughed, my mother shushed them with an iron stare.
MILTON BERLE

Attend as many of your child's or teen's
school events as possible.
If he is in a play, an athletic event, or musical event,
be there. He may not say, "Thanks for coming,"
but he always looks for you!

50

I have held many things in my hands
and I have lost them all;
But whatever I placed in God's hands,
that I still possess.

What things, people, or desires do you need to give
to God today? The safest place for what is dearest
to your heart is in God's hands.

51

A mother is not a person to lean on
but a person to make leaning unnecessary.
DOROTHY CANFIELD FISHER

Give your child daily or weekly chores (according to
his or her age) that facilitate the smooth running of
the household. Write the chores down and don't do
them when your child fails to follow through. That
way you build a sense of belonging, of being needed,
and you help your child learn valuable life skills.

52

My mother had a great deal of trouble with me,
but I think she enjoyed it.
MARK TWAIN

When you have trouble with your teen,
discuss it with a person you can trust. Get help
to deal with the immediate problem, make a plan
of action, and request support so you can go on
"enjoying" your child while working on the problem.

53

A cheerful heart is good medicine,
but a crushed spirit dries up the bones.
PROVERBS 17:22 (NIV)

Tickle *your* funny bone by going to a comedy movie
or looking for humorous comic strips in the
newspaper. Share your fun with the family.

54

Since children learn the most by imitation,
they need models rather than critics.

Think about the behaviors and attitudes you model in
your daily lifestyle. Ultimately, that is what your child
will follow. Write down one area where you would like
to be a better role model and brainstorm how you will
change that behavior or attitude.

55

Although most moms hope for an "easy" baby, the fact is that
most perfectly healthy babies are not easy—they have bouts
of crying that can pose quite a challenge.[1]

Here are some ways to cope with a baby
who cries a lot:
▶ Don't take on a lot of guilt; it's not your fault.
▶ Speak softly to baby and move gently
when holding her.
▶ Find a moms' support group at a local church.
▶ Remember, this too shall pass! After three months,
much fussiness subsides. In the meantime, get Dad
to take over one night so you can get some sleep!

56

Tie the child to you, and the child will either run away or turn into a stone. Give the child wings, and the child will use them to fly back to you.
ANGELA BARRON MCBRIDE,
THE SECRET OF A GOOD LIFE WITH YOUR TEENAGER

Let your teen know you are preparing him for when he will be on his own. Teach him how to manage money by helping him open a checking account or how to deal with his own responsibilities and mistakes by not rushing down to the high school with the research paper or lunch money he forgot.

57

Too many people put off something that brings them joy just because they didn't have it on their schedule, didn't know it was coming, or are too rigid to depart from the routine.
ERMA BOMBECK,
UNITED PRESS SYNDICATE

When your teen says, "Let's go get a hamburger!" or "Let's stay up together, pop some popcorn, and watch an old movie," or "Let's go to the lake and rollerblade!" *seize the moment* (especially if you have rollerblades) and enjoy the time together.
Instead of giving excuses, do it now!

58

Youth has one great element in its favor—
it can live in the future.
HENRY FORD

Talk with your teen about the future.
What are her hopes and dreams? How can you help
her plan and set goals, both in taking courses at school
and getting experience in the community, that will
lead her where she wants to go?

59

When you understand third-grade math, you don't belong
in third-grade math classes. If we understood what
parenthood has to teach us, we wouldn't belong in
parenthood. If we understood how to be perfect spouses,
we probably wouldn't belong in marriage. . . . If we
understood our oneness with God we probably wouldn't need
churches. Jeremiah envisioned such a day, "When no one
shall teach his neighbor saying, 'know ye the Lord,' for they
shall know me, from the least of them to the greatest."
Meanwhile, thank goodness for the learning.
POLLY BERRIEN BERENDS

Try to capture in a few sentences what God
is teaching you at this stage of parenthood
and marriage. Thank Him for the learning process
and His patience as you grow at the usual pace
of three steps forward and two steps back.

60

The art of being wise is the art
of knowing what to overlook.
WILLIAM JAMES

Make a practice of overlooking your child's faults
and focus on what she is doing *right* today.

61

A precious deposit a parent can give her child is the gift of her
own voice, the treasure of her own favorite songs and stories.

Record your voice reading favorite books or telling
stories to your child. Conclude the tape by singing
some family songs. Let your child take the tape to
Grandma's overnight or listen to it at nap or bedtime
when you have to be away.

62

Knowledge is experience—
everything else is just information.
ALBERT EINSTEIN

When your child is learning abstract concepts,
let him learn experientially and concretely,
approaching it in a hands-on way: Cut one candy bar
into three parts to find out what one-third means,
dissect flowers while learning about the reproductive
system of plants, or help him set up a Saturday
lemonade stand so he can learn to count money.

63

SOMETIMES . . . let's just blow bubbles,
For no good reason, let's just blow bubbles.
Laugh a little, watch them disappear. . . .
Smile and touch the rainbow colors,
watch them float in air.
RUTH REARDON,
LISTEN TO THE LITTLEST

For a lively bubble-blowing mixture: Mix one-fourth
cup dishwashing liquid with three-fourths cup of
water, and add one or two teaspoons of glycerin.
You can use a coat hanger bent into a circle for huge
bubbles, the plastic top of a cola six-pack for six
bubbles at a time, or other interesting objects to blow
the bubbles. Have fun!

64

*Music gives . . . wings to the mind, flight to the imagination,
a charm to sadness, gaiety and life to everything.*
PLATO

Tune in to a classical music station as a background
for part of your home and car time together—classical
music is a wonderful backdrop for any work from bill
paying to carpooling, cooking to household chores.

65

*Mother's Day is that happy time when your child says, "I
love you" or "Thank you" or "You're a great mom!"*

Select a favorite card you've received from your child
on a past Mother's Day or your birthday.
Frame and hang it in your bedroom.

66

It is better to build children than to mend adults.

In what ways can you *build* your child today? In what
ways can you build his sense of security by spending
time together, his moral sense by reading aloud some
proverbs or a story from *The Book of Virtues*, his self-
esteem by praising him for his effort in school?

67

We always had someone living with our family—an aunt, a nephew, an exchange student. It kept our family system an open one instead of a closed one, and our children grew up conscious that they could care for other people, offer a helping hand, or even bring them home.

PATTY JOHNSTON,
FROM AN INTERVIEW

Open your home by:
► inviting a foreign-exchange student to dinner
(call a local college for names);
► having out-of-town nieces or nephews come
for a regular summer visit;
► picking a consistent evening each week
to have a guest for dinner.

68

Today's world differs from the world we knew as children. We cannot determine our children's feelings based on our childhood experiences, which grew out of an environment different from our children's.

DR. W. GEORGE SELIG

By daily conversations with your children, by involving yourself in a hands-on way in their world of school, Scouts, and other activities, you can gain insight on how their environment impacts them. You need to be alert to the pressures, changing mood, and demands of the present culture and what you can do to facilitate your child's growth in the midst of it.

69

Many women suffer from "Hurry Sickness."
Bruce Baldwin describes the symptoms as: a constant sense
of time urgency, inability to relax, the tendency to finish other
people's sentences even during recreation or making love, and
impatience with drivers and others who aren't on as fast a
track as they are.

Discuss as a family: Do I know how to relax?
Do I make time to parachute down from the day's
events in the evening? Do I model for you how
to "get away from it all," to laugh, recreate, and be
rejuvenated, or am I constantly hurrying myself
and rushing you?

70

The best and most beautiful things in the world cannot be
seen or even touched. They must be felt with the heart.
HELEN KELLER

What are the best and most beautiful things in your
world? List them in your journal, thank God for them,
and make time to appreciate and enjoy them. Discuss
your "best and beautiful" list at the dinner table,
asking each person to mention something that would
appear on his or her list.

71

Make new friends but keep the old,
One is silver, the other's gold.

Send a yearly Christmas letter to your "golden" friends. Tell the highlight events of your family, month by month; the special things God has done in your lives; and share a blessing for their family. Have your kids contribute information, illustrate the letter, and sign it. This is a great way to show your children how to continue relationships even from long distance.

72

He who cannot give anything away
cannot feel anything either.
FRIEDRICH W. NIETZSCHE

At the close of each season, go through your family's closets to find those things (clothes, toys, etc.) that are in good shape, yet outgrown or unused, and can be lovingly given to the Salvation Army or a local homeless shelter. Take your child with you when you drop off your contributions.

73

The difference between the right word and the almost right word is really a large matter—it's the difference between lightning and the lightning bug.
**MARK TWAIN,
"LETTER TO GEORGE BAINTON," 1888**

Work on your family's "word smarts" by
keeping a dictionary handy to look up words
and their definitions, by working crossword puzzles
or by playing word games like Scrabble,
and by reading voraciously.

74

Attitude, to me, is more important than facts. It is more important than the past, than education, than money, than circumstances, than failures, than successes, than what other people think or say or do. It is more important than appearance, giftedness, or skill. The remarkable thing is we have a choice every day regarding the attitude we will embrace for that day.
**CHUCK SWINDOLL,
"INSIGHT FOR LIVING"**

Have a periodic "Attitude Check" at your house when
strife and frustrations build. Play lively music in the
morning to promote a positive attitude to start the day.
Encourage your children to focus on the positive,
to look at problems as opportunities, and to learn
something from every trial or challenge.

75

*Opportunity is missed by most people because
it is dressed in overalls and looks like work.*
THOMAS EDISON

Teach your children good work habits and attitudes.
Emphasize that work is a gift. We do all our tasks
as if we are doing them for God and we always
finish the job we start.

76

*No one is immune to problems.
Even the lion has to fight off flies.*

Are you perfectionistic? Remember that there are
no perfect moms—all parents and children have
problems from time to time. In fact, the only perfect
parent was God, and look what problems He faced
with His children, Adam and Eve! When you face a
problem, brainstorm as a family for possible solutions.
Help your children see that facing and solving
problems together is one of the best ways
to grow closer to God and to each other.

77

Our duty is not to gaze at what lies dimly at a distance,
but to do what lies clearly at hand.
THOMAS CARLYLE

What task or unfinished business have you been
putting off or avoiding but could do *today*? Do you
need to write an overdue thank-you note or clean out
a closet? Do it today.

78

Family newsletters can foster a connectedness
between reunions. Even more important, they help kids
develop a sense of belonging. Children realize they have ties
to different sizes, shapes, and kinds of people, not just their
family unit. It also provides them models that inspire them to
achievement—the cousin who wins a scholarship to study in
Germany, the aunt who succeeds at her own business. "Yes, I
could do that! My family does these things."

Create a newsletter for extended family
and give it a unique name (for example, "Heath
Herald" or "Taylor Tidings"). Gather news about
everything from new babies to little cousins' soccer
championships, from aunt's travel plans to news of
pets, weddings, college kids' course loads, and the
next reunion plans. Have family members help in the
process: one can call to get news items, one can type
the newsletter, another can copy and mail it out.
A great way to boost family ties, this newsletter
can be sent out several times a year.

79

*Mothers bring rays of sunshine and the fragrance
of flowers to lighten our hearts in discouraging hours.*

Gather some bright pansies, clover, goldenrod, and
other flowers and share with your child the old-
fashioned fun of flower pressing:
> ► Choose flowers that can lie flat and look
> for variety in color and size.
> ► Pick the flowers late in the day so they are
> free of dew.
► Put a piece of clear wax paper in a phone book or
heavy book with the flowers inside.
► Close and place a heavy brick on top. Leave for two
weeks in a dry place and then the dry,
pressed flowers are ready to enjoy
even on rainy or wintry days.

80

*Everybody suffers from negativism and bad days at times.
Positive reminders can promote a fresh perspective
and a persevering "can-do" attitude,
even during the most difficult times.*

Collect and post winning statements on your child's
wall or bulletin such as, "Don't give up. Keep going.
There's always a chance you will stumble onto
something terrific! I've never heard of anyone
stumbling over anything while he was sitting down."

81

The best security blanket a child can have
is parents who respect each other.
JAN BLAUSTONE

Show respect for your mate by using a kind tone
of voice and by respecting differences of opinion.

82

A good example is like a bell that calls many to church.
DANISH PROVERB

Think about all the ways you can be a good example
to your children today: Wear your seatbelt, be an avid
reader and an enthusiastic learner, and live out before
them in small, daily ways the values you hold dear
and hope to pass on to them.

83

Hide not your talents.
They for use were made.
What's a sundial in the shade?
BENJAMIN FRANKLIN

Look for your children's talents and let them know
that what they do is important to you. Does he write
poetry? You can say, "Let me read your newest
poems." Does she paint, play tennis, or like to invent
new gadgets? Encourage her developing skills and
gifts and give her opportunities to use them at home,
church, and school.

84

*The most important thing in communication
is to hear what isn't being said.*
**PETER F. DRUCKER,
QUOTED IN *A WORLD OF IDEAS***

When your child won't talk about her feelings,
look at her art and drawings. In trying times kids can
use paint and markers to communicate fear, joy,
sadness, and worry.

85

*What is a hero? A hero goes beyond mere fame
and serves something larger than themselves. Heroes live
lives worthy of imitation; they are catalysts for positive
change. Thomas Jefferson. Rosa Parks. Albert Schweitzer.
I think Jesus is the ultimate hero.*
**LOUIS LOTZ,
"WHERE HAVE ALL OUR HEROES GONE?"**

Help your child discover *true heroes* (not just
the superstar athletes and Hollywood stars) in history
and even in the community around you: the cancer
patient who serves the elderly in his neighborhood
until the end, the single mom without a car who
makes huge sacrifices to support her child's education
and takes him to church every Sunday, the state
senator who takes a stand for right although it costs
her votes. Collect stories about these people
of courage and determination; save them
in a "Heroes File" and read them aloud.

86

For each one of us there is a special gift,
the way in which we may best serve and please
the Lord whose love is so overflowing.
MADELEINE L'ENGLE,
WALKING ON WATER

Help your child identify his or her spiritual gift.
Is it teaching? Compassion? Service? Administration?
Leadership? Creativity? Find ways for both of you
to use your spiritual gifts in your family,
community, and church.

87

The best way to prepare your children for the future
is to hide God's Word in their hearts.

Have your child write a Bible verse for the week on a
slip of paper. Then stick it in a balloon and inflate it.
When he can successfully say the verse, he gets to pop
the balloon and tack the verse on his calendar.

88

Behind every great kid is a great family.

For the next family reunion,
personalize T-shirts for each child. Using
bright paint pens or embroidery, write the quote
"Behind every great kid is a great family," and let every
child draw his own scene of cousins, rainbows,
sunshine, or other decoration and symbols.

89

*One of the best ways to encourage your child's creativity
is to show him you value his "creations"!*

If you have collected your children's artwork
for years and are running out of space for storing it,
or it's taking over your house, collect all the paintings,
lumpy sculptures, potholders, and collages, and make
a lasting record of the creations on *videotape*.
This prevents your children from thinking
you don't like the treasures.

90

Learning stamps you with its moments. Childhood's learning is made up of moments. It isn't steady. It's a pulse.
EUDORA WELTY,
ONE WRITER'S BEGINNINGS

Seize moments with your child to gaze at the velvety black night sky, to stick just-picked yellow daffodils in a vase and paint them on drawing paper, to curl up on the fluffy comforter and read delightful books aloud. In the long run, these activities can have far greater impact than classroom learning.

91

A miracle happens to the person whose self-esteem has been raised. He suddenly likes other people better. He is kinder and more cooperative with those around him. Praise is the polish that helps keep his self-image bright and sparkling.
GOTTFRIED R. VON KRONENBERGER,
"WORDS THAT WORK MIRACLES"

Boost your child's self-esteem by telling him that
▶ he is made in the image of God;
▶ God has a purpose for his life, something he can do better than 10,000 other people;
▶ God has gifted him with the talents and intelligence to fulfill that purpose.

92

Traditions are formed subtly,
sometimes without our realizing it.
An experience that brings such joy
that we want to repeat in the same way
soon becomes a family custom.

We began a birthday tradition in our family when I decorated a chair with balloons, crepe paper, and a bright banner. The first thing seen in the morning, the decorated chair was the birthday child's "throne" to sit in for meals that day. From then on, the kids thought no birthday was complete without a Birthday Chair.

93

A teacher touches a life forever.

Encourage one of your child's teachers by writing a note of thanks and giving it with a small loaf of fruit bread, brownies, or a bright inspirational poster for her classroom.

94

Friendship cheers like a sunbeam; charms like a good story;
inspires like a brave leader; binds like a golden chain;
guides like a heavenly vision.
NEWELL D. HILLIS

Plan a moms' night out once a month: Get together
with a few friends for a potluck supper and board
game, walk the mall and stop for tea and talk,
or work on quilting and crafts together. This builds
friendships and dissolves loneliness.

95

Character is not an inheritance;
each person must build it for himself.

Build character in your child by discussing a different
virtue each week: respect for others, kindness to pets,
perseverance, service and help to others. Read a story
about that character quality and brainstorm ways
to demonstrate the quality in everyday life.

96

*Laughter is the key to survival during the special stresses
of the childrearing years. If you can see the delightful side
of your assignment, you can also deal with the difficult.*
DR. JAMES DOBSON,
PARENTING ISN'T FOR COWARDS

When you see family or work situations as humorous,
share it with your kids! Consider bringing daily family
"funnies" to the dinner table as well as riddles,
amusing headlines, and silly stories.

97

*Forgiveness saves the expense of anger,
the cost of hatred, and the waste of energy.*

Make it a family tradition never to go to bed angry
at anyone in the family. Bedtime prayer is a good time
to broach the subject, especially if there's been a
conflict between siblings or between child and parent.
Encourage talking it over, forgiving the person out
loud, and hugging and making up before
the light goes out!

98

A family should have a whole museum of memories gathered through the years—collections of carefully preserved memories and a realization that day-by-day memories are being chosen for our museum. . . . That time can be made to have double value by recognizing that what is done today will be tomorrow's memory.

EDITH SHAEFFER,
WHAT IS A FAMILY?

Take a photograph of your family doing a favorite activity. Blow up the photo to an eight-by-ten size or larger and make it into a puzzle for your child to put together and also remember a happy time together.

99

At times children can be God's sandpaper grating against your nerves and wishes, but at other times they are like a healing medicine that God pours over your soul.

In what way is your child "heavenly sandpaper" at this stage and age? In a quiet moment write down what's grating against your nerves, yield it to God, and ask Him for the grace to accept your child and the wisdom to know how to handle his behavior!

100

Sooner or later our kids want to know what our childhood was like, how we celebrated Christmas, how we were disciplined, what fads we followed. Sadly, it's often after our parents are gone when we think of those questions. So I wrote my life and gave it to our grown children as a legacy— a one-of-a-kind gift that only a parent can give.
DOROTHY BURSHEK

As you write your life story, use memory joggers— photos, family Bibles, old letters—to prime the pump; start writing memories as they come and later organize them chronologically or by subject (these become chapters); and enjoy the writing process now by editing later.

101

In our society, at the age of five, 90 percent of the population measures "high creativity." By the age of seven, the figure has dropped to 10 percent, and by adulthood it is only 2 percent.[2]

Keep your child's creativity high by
► Providing the raw materials of invention, art supplies of all kinds, buttons and pipe cleaners, Styrofoam trays, collage materials, and glue;
► Providing a table to create things and leave the materials out, and by giving lots of encouragement;
► Looking at things in new ways.

102

*The walks and talks we have with our two-year-olds
in red boots have a great deal to do with the values
they will cherish as adults.*
EDITH F. HUNTER

Take time for walks together around the block
on a sunny day, to splash in puddles on rainy days,
or to walk and talk by a lake
where you can feed the ducks.

103

Adventure is worthwhile in itself.
AMELIA EARHART

Talk with your child about an adventure he's always
wanted to have: climbing a mountain, an overnight
hike, or whatever his definition of "adventure" is.
Help him plan how to reach that goal.
Encourage him to read about it, save toward it,
and look forward to pursuing that adventure.

104

Every good gift is meant to be shared. Whether it's a delicious recipe, a packet of marigold seeds from my bountiful garden blooms . . . or God's wonderful plan of salvation.
DOROTHY SHELLENBERGER,
FROM AN INTERVIEW

Pray "Dear Lord, where would I be without the love-gift of Yourself? Help me to realize that selfishness is deadly and show me a good gift You've given me that I could share with someone else today."

105

Every person that you meet, every experience that God gives you is preparation for the future, which only He can see.
CORRIE TEN BOOM,
FROM AN INTERVIEW

Write in your journal about an experience that prepared you for something you're doing today or write about someone you've been able to minister to and comfort as a result of past experiences God has taken you through.

106

*Talking dolls and electronic gadgets may get lost or broken,
but memories, especially those of warmth and togetherness,
last for a lifetime. They give children a sense of belonging
and continuity that money can't buy.*

Save in a file some important mementos—
things that reflect important and delightful family
times, school experiences and awards, special greeting
cards and little "collectibles" your children have
received from friends or relatives. At the end of each
year, transfer each child's mementos to a box she or he
has covered with fabric or decorative paper. Bring out
the boxes on a rainy day or a sick-in-bed day and let
your child sort through the memories.

107

Happy is the house that shelters a friend.

Let your house be a place in which your child's friends
feel comfortable. Welcome them when they arrive.
Ask questions about their lives.
Include them for lunch, dinner,
or an occasional overnight stay.

108

*One of the best ways to motivate your child
is to let her "eavesdrop" on your positive comments
about her to someone else.*

If your child were to overhear your conversations
about her, what would she hear? Comments that
would give her *confidence* or comments that would
discourage her? Think about the positive things you
can say about your child to someone else today—
either in person or on the phone. Talk about how she's
improving in an area, how she was kind
to a classmate, or whatever else you notice about her.

109

*Every day should be distinguished
by at least one particular act of love.*
JOHANN KASPAR LAVATER

Extend a little lovingkindness to someone each day. Is
there a shut-in or someone recovering from sickness
whom you could call and check on? Is there a single
person in your neighborhood you could invite to
dinner tonight? How about fixing your husband's
favorite entree or taking special un-rushed time
to read a book to your child at bedtime?

110

Learn to say "No";
It will be of more use to you
than to be able to read Latin.
CHARLES HADDON SPURGEON

List your scheduled activities. Then list your top four
priorities in life. Which activities sap your time and
lead you away from what's really important to you and
your children? Practice graciously saying *no* to
activities that are good but keep you from God's best.

111

How you'll be in twenty years is the sum total
of the friends you associate with, the books you read,
and the music you listen to.
MAX LUCADO, "UP WORDS" RADIO BROADCAST

Take a closer look at your bookshelves, music,
entertainment, and friends. Are the values they reflect
what you want to be aiming for? We can't choose the
family who brought us into this world, but we can
choose the mentors who lead us through this world.

112

Worry doesn't empty tomorrow of its sorrows.
It empties today of its strength.
CORRIE TEN BOOM

Empty out any worries you have today concerning
finances, children, health, or other family members.
In your mind's eye, think of pouring them all out,
as from a pitcher, right at the feet of Jesus.
Now let your pitcher refill with His peace and love.

113

Smile! It takes thirty-four muscles to frown
and only thirteen to smile. Why make the extra effort?[3]

When children are small and have bad attitudes,
have them go to the kitchen, open a particular
cupboard drawer, and pull out an imaginary smile to
put on. The foolishness of the action almost always
turns a frown upside-down.

114

Hatred stirs up dissension, but love covers over all wrongs.
PROVERBS 10:12 (NIV)

Pray for "love that covers" your spouse's faults
and mistakes, and for eyes to see the best in him.

115

Learning is not attained by chance.
It must be sought for with ardor and attended to
with diligence.
ABIGAIL ADAMS,
LETTER TO JOHN QUINCY ADAMS, 1780

Establish a daily study time with your school-age
children in which they have a set amount of time for
homework, reading (either for school or from your
home reading list) and/or working ahead on long-term
assignments such as science or history projects. Begin
with a shorter amount of time for younger children.

116

We all have glimpses of glory as children, and as we grow up
we forget them, or are taught to think we made them up.
MADELEINE L'ENGLE,
WALKING ON WATER

Write down your young child's "glimpses of glory"
as she shares them either in story, pictures, or songs—
those special insights about the happenings and
people around you, what she thinks about God,
nature, and people.

117

"Be strong and courageous. Do not be terrified;
do not be discouraged, for the LORD your God
will be with you wherever you go."
JOSHUA 1:9 (NIV)

Read to your child the story of Joshua and the battle
of Jericho from a Bible storybook. Discuss how God
was with Joshua and helped him lead the Israelites
to accomplish impossible things. Assist your child in
overcoming one fear this week by helping him identify
the fear (for a young child, drawing a picture of the
fear helps) and pray for courage and trust in God.
Memorize Joshua 1:9 together.

118

Never before in the history of the world has the spirit of
giving been as needed as it is today. There is so much that
every one of us, no matter how great or how modest our
talents . . . can quietly do in the routine of our lives to cure
at least some of the ills of our troubled times.
DAVID DUNN, *TRY GIVING YOURSELF AWAY*

Make a list of ways you and your kids can "give
yourself away" and choose one
to put into action today:
► Make a meal or banana bread for someone
who is sick.
► Visit someone in a nearby nursing home.
► Offer to keep a young mother's child
so she can get out for an afternoon.

119

Come apart before you come a-part.

Find a few quiet moments at the start of the day,
even if you have to get up before everyone else, to sip
a cup of tea and read a devotional, to say "Good
morning" to your Heavenly Father, and to give
the day and your plans to Him.

120

*As moms we tend to worship God in solitude (if we have any
solitude!) and our children never get to see us having special
time with God. And then there are those times when days
start with a bang and they get up before we do,
so there is no "quiet" time with Him.*

CONNIE BAKER,
FROM AN INTERVIEW

Make your own "Mobile Quiet Time Unit" by
assembling on a tray a Bible and study book; a
calendar (to jot down "things to do" that jump into
your mind and distract you); a prayer journal; and
stationery. When your children are small and you need
to be where they are, your "Mobile Quiet Time Unit"
can go wherever they play, and you can enjoy a few
moments to pray or read your Bible. Your children
may even run and get their own Bibles to join you!

121

Your word is a lamp to my feet and a light for my path.
PSALM 119:105 (NIV)

Pray for your children when you pair their socks;
pray that God will always guide their steps
and light their paths.

122

*Think of giving your child independence as being
like reel-fishing. You let out just a little line at a time.
The struggle is less; the line doesn't break; and eventually
you do get to keep the fish.*
**NANCY HULSHULT,
FROM AN INTERVIEW**

Write down two ways you can "let the line out a little"
in your child's life this week. Is there something he
could do for himself that you are doing for him? Is
there a household job you could teach him to do that
would build his sense of being capable and helpful?

123

Take a moment to listen today
to what your children are trying to say.
Listen today, whatever you do
And they will come back to listen to you.

Here's how to improve your listening ability:
- ►Look at your child and pay attention
to words and body language.
- ►Be available to talk, even about sensitive subjects,
without overreacting.
- ►When your child wants to talk and you are busy
or can't give full attention, explain why you can't listen
right now and set a time for later.
- ►Silently pray for her and ask God to put
His thoughts in your mind and show you how
to respond to what she says.

124

What good news it is that our very inadequacy
is the master key swinging wide the door to His adequacy.
Forever and forever our hunger drives us to "taste and see
that the Lord is good." Who but Jesus could ever have
thought of a plan like that!
CATHERINE MARSHALL, ADVENTURES IN PRAYER

Do you have a great or small need today and
insufficient resources of your own to meet it?
Give God your inadequacy and receive His provision
and strength for whatever need you face.

125

Humor diffuses stress in a family,
pulls bricks out of the walls that come between us,
and helps us remember why we liked each other
in the first place.

KAY BISHOP,
FROM AN INTERVIEW

Want your home to be a place of laughter?
► Try sending a funny card to your spouse or child.
► Laugh at your child's spontaneous jokes and riddles.
► Try not to take yourself and your problems
so seriously.
► Keep a Funny Book—humorous things
your kids have said and done!

126

Children do not develop self-esteem or mature
if they are not loved. And don't assume they know how much
you love them; let them know every day!

Say "I love you" to your child regularly—on days
when she's pleasant and on days when she's moody
and crabby; on days when she makes a lower grade
than usual or doesn't win a gymnastics match.

127

Lullaby CD's and other recorded music collections are great, but they can't replace a mother's voice as she sings her little one to sleep or soothes a fever.

When your baby is fussy and needs calming, when you diaper and feed and care for her, or when she's riding in the car while you go about your day, sing favorite nursery rhymes and make up your own melodies that tell her, "You are my joy, my sunshine!"

128

Moral expectations without explanation will lead to exasperation.
KIM AND ERIC BUEHRER,
GATEWAYS REPORT

Develop a Family Code of Honor. On paper, capture in one sentence your expectations for your children in how they conduct themselves. Areas of attitude and behavior can cover such diverse areas as honesty, responsibility, homework; and for older kids, dating, smoking, friends. Discuss this as a family and post the Code of Honor in a visible place.

129

"Life" is what happens
when you're making other plans.
FLO PERKINS,
FROM AN INTERVIEW

Be prepared for the "unexpected":
Carry a first-aid kit and a "survival" kit in the car
on all trips and outings. The survival kit could consist
of a small calculator, stickers, colored pieces of paper,
fluorescent markers, sticky notes, a small book,
magnifying glass, etc. It will keep your child occupied
during an unexpected wait at the doctor's office
or an extra-long errand. The first-aid kit can be kept
in a Zip-Lock bag and contain Band-Aids, antiseptic
in small sterile packets, insect repellent,
and an anti-itch cream such as Caladryl.

130

Babies are always more trouble than you thought—
and more wonderful.
CHARLES OSGOOD

You'll get more done if you meet your baby's or young
child's needs *before* you do telephone or desk work for
your home business, church, or volunteer job. Hug
him, read to him, play with him, or just listen to him
and fill his emotional tank (and tummy if needed).
Then tackle your tasks.

131

Organizing is what you do before you do something,
so that when you do it, it's not all mixed up.
A. A. MILNE

Help your child get organized
by the following methods:
▶ Provide a big calendar in her room to record due
dates for school projects, upcoming activities,
and weekly piano/dance/karate lessons.
▶ Provide a "school box" by the door for gloves,
backpack (with a designated pouch for completed
homework), Show & Tell material,
and gym or sports clothes.
▶ Teach your child how to organize clothes in labeled
drawers and hang clothes on color-coded hangers for
easy access.

132

One must ask children and birds how cherries
and strawberries taste.
GOETHE

Put pieces of fruit—cherries, strawberries, sliced kiwi,
your child's favorite fruit—in a sack. Have her close
her eyes, draw a piece out, and taste it. Ask her to tell
you what each taste is. Then make a fruit pizza
together and enjoy.

133

A blessing gives clarity and focus to what is happening at the table. Of all the things you give your children, the family meal is one of the most precious. . . . Prayer shows thanks that everything is with God's permission. Everything we do is an act of worship, even eating. We eat what is of God's goodness. The blessing keeps us mindful of that.

BARBARA DANIEL

Keep your mealtime prayer a special time:
►Hold hands as you pray.
►Let each family member say a sentence
or two of thanks to God.
►Sing the evening prayer. Pick a familiar melody
and thank God for the food and your blessings
in a song.

134

The first weeks of school set the tone for the rest of the year. Make it a positive time and your child will have a much better chance to succeed.

When you start the school year, hit the discount or grocery store for the following items, and pack them in a zippered three-ring pencil bag that fits in your child's notebook. Write a note to explain each item. Here are some ideas:
►An eraser in the shape of a star:
Jesus shines through you!
►Lifesaver mints:
Be a lifesaver to someone who needs a little help.
►Pencil with a message like "You're tops!"

135

According to Dr. Jean Lush, 71 percent of women think the world is out of control. We're concerned about our children, grandchildren, spouses, and friends. And we try to press more into our twenty-four-hour day than is humanly possible. It all takes a toll on us physically and emotionally.[4]

If you are in the middle of a stressful time,
try to tame the tension in these ways:
- Ventilate—talk with a friend about
what's burdening or bothering.
- Whistle a tune or play music and sing along.
- Strive for excellence, *not* perfection.
- Take a bubble bath before bedtime.
- Save some time each day to play with your child
(or even patty-cake with your toddler).

136

We spend one-fifth of our lives talking and speak enough words in one year to fill sixty-six books, each eight hundred pages long! The average woman speaks thirty thousand words a day; and the more you talk, the greater the chance your words will get you into trouble.[5]

Here are some ways to be wise with your words:
- Think *before* you speak. (If angry, count to ten!)
- Speak the truth in *love*.
- Ask the Holy Spirit to help you speak words
that build others up and to control the thoughts
behind your words. For "out of the abundance
of the heart, the mouth speaks."

137

Judging and criticizing other parents for their schooling choices brings division and discouragement and the children are the losers. But when we support each other's decisions for schooling, the kids are the beneficiaries!

▶ Look for ways to help and encourage families in school situations different from your own.
▶ Pray for wisdom for the parents, because *all* schooling has problems.
▶ Show interest in another's schooling choices by asking questions about progress and activities.

138

If Jesus Christ faced you squarely with the question, "What do you want?" what would you ask Him to do for you? Then think of your children. What would you want Jesus to do for each of them? What request should you make for them?

JEAN FLEMING, A MOTHER'S HEART

During your quiet time, make prayers of those verses that converge with your child's needs and your hopes for him. For example:
▶ 1 Chronicles 29:19—
"Give my son a good heart toward You, God, so that he will want to obey you in the smallest detail."
▶ Proverbs 2:20—
"Lord, protect him from friends who would lead him in the wrong direction; give him the right friends who would encourage him to excel and follow You."

139

An idea is a fragile thing.
Don't turn it off.

If your child has a "bright idea" this week,
think about how you can turn it *on* instead of turning
it off. If there's no time to work on it today, have your
child write it on an index card and tack it on the
bulletin board under "Things to Do." You could also
brainstorm about the materials she would need to
carry out her idea and then take her to the library
to get more information.

140

Suppressed hurts and wounds sap our energy and cause us
to be emotionally inaccessible to our children and spouse.
Remember: There is no hurt too deep for God to heal.

Write down your recent and not-so-recent hurts
and the people who caused them. Give these wounds
to God and forgive each person
and then forgive yourself.
If necessary, get counsel from a trusted friend
or professional.

141

Although I may not walk with kings,
Let me be big in little things.
EDGAR GUEST

It's not the big things that create happiness and
security for a child; it's the day-to-day accumulation of
little things like special pancakes with whipped cream
on an un-holiday; a surprise trip to the amusement
park, playing catch in the backyard. Be faithful to
fulfill the little promises you make to your child.

142

Financial responsibility is one of the greatest gifts
we can give to our children. To assume a young child is
unable to understand the basic principles of saving, giving,
and limiting spending to current resources is to miss
a wonderful opportunity to instill practical values
that will last a lifetime.
MARY HUNT, *CHEAPSKATE MONTHLY NEWSLETTER*

►Give your kids a "salary."
Mary suggests it be paid weekly or monthly.
►They must save 10 percent, give away 10 percent,
and decide how to spend the other 80 percent
on some of their expenses and wants.
►Let them make financial mistakes
and learn from them.
►As you continue in this way, you'll gradually
replace their "youthful dependence with self-reliance"
and a far greater gift than money itself—
the ability to manage it wisely![6]

143

Gratitude is a memory of the heart.

Every Thanksgiving, write a letter of appreciation
to your husband, children, and parents, telling them
what you've learned from them in the past year, how
you've been blessed by their support, and how you've
been enriched by your relationship with them.

144

A word of encouragement does wonders!
PROVERBS 12:25, PARAPHRASE

Remember and notice the good things
your child does. On a regular basis, substitute
phrases such as, "You really are growing up" or "doing
a great job on your homework"; substitute "I really
appreciate your . . . (humor, perseverance, kindness)"
for critical words. Then watch your child's
motivation and confidence rise!

145

Life is short and then it's past,
Only what's done for Christ will last.

Teach your children to consult with God about
everything—activities, lessons, sports, friends. And
train them to pray from an early age about college,
career, and a life partner.

146

A goal is a dream set within a time frame.
DOROTHY LEHMKUHL,
ORGANIZING FOR THE CREATIVE PERSON

Help your child set goals for each week, month, and
year. Write down the goals in categories such as
academic, spiritual, talent, or sports skill development,
etc. Pray with him as he commits his plans to God.
Then help him break the goals into steps
and encourage him to go for it!

147

You'll never eliminate all stress from your life.
You wouldn't want to. But you can reduce the intensity
of stress and you can learn to manage it—
and the best way is to recharge spiritually.
RICK WARREN, FAX OF LIFE

If you are experiencing stress today:
- ► Take a spiritual break—focusing on God, quieting yourself and thanking Him that He is *with you.*
- ► Pray aloud, if possible, and tell God how you feel and what you need.
- ► Prioritize your time for the rest of the day or week. Do the important and not just the urgent things.

148

Neither a borrower nor a lender be.
SHAKESPEARE, HAMLET

Whether it's a book or a cup of sugar, we all borrow at some time. When you do borrow,
- ► keep a list of what you borrowed (tack it to your bulletin board);
- ► return it promptly and in even better shape than when you got it;
- ► teach your children to do the same.

149

How can a young person live a clean life?
By carefully reading the map of your Word.
PSALM 119:9 (*THE MESSAGE*)

When your child is capable of reading
a children's Bible (usually first or second grade),
have a family ceremony to present him with a Bible
engraved with his name. Begin the ceremony by
encouraging him to read God's Word every day. Then
sing a song together, give your child a blessing related
to reading the Bible, and present the Bible to him. Let
him read a passage for the family right then. Invite
grandparents, aunts, and close family friends
and serve cookies and juice afterward.

150

Good is the most contagious virus.
One person's good behavior spawns more good.

Think of some acts of goodness you could perform
today. For instance, you could smile at everybody you
meet, let an older driver take the parking place you
had planned to take, call someone whom you know is
feeling down, wave at people in your neighborhood.
Let someone "catch" the "virus" of goodness
from you.

151

A teacher affects eternity;
she can never tell where her influence stops.

Next time you're at the grocery store, buy one of the
following (or come up with your own gift) and attach
a small note to it with bright curly ribbon to show
appreciation to your child's teacher:
- ▶ Votive candle: Your light shines brightly
and we are grateful for you!
- ▶ Tall decorative fireplace matches: Your teaching is
creative and really fires up your students!
- ▶ Fifth Avenue candy bar: Your teaching would stand
out on Fifth Avenue! Thanks for all you do
for our kids!

152

Do you love me
Or do you not?
You told me once
But I forgot.

When was the last time you told your husband you
love him? Try communicating your love in creative
ways. Would he "hear" and receive your love best if
you say it with physical affection—maybe a hug or
just sitting close to him during a televised football
game? Is he a word person who likes to hear words
of admiration or even read them in a card? Is he a giver
who would love to receive a thoughtful present—
a new pair of boxer shorts or a box of golf balls?

153

The caffeine and sugar mix many moms use to beat their afternoon slump is a stressor that makes their bodies feel worse in the long run. Caffeine causes restlessness, headache, insomnia, a racing heartbeat—and another big slump an hour later.

Instead of grabbing a Diet Coke and some chocolate to refuel in the afternoon, beat your mid-afternoon slump with a short walk and fresh fruit or another healthy snack.

154

As our children grow and we gradually lose direct control— as their wings get stronger and they begin to fly out of the nest for short flights and then to college and beyond, our prayers are the wind beneath their wings.

Whether your teen is pleasing you or disappointing you with his choices and behavior, whether he is achieving or not achieving, persevere in prayer for *heart changes*—for his affections to turn from the world to Christ—and for his protection from bad choices that will affect his future.

155

Everybody is ignorant . . . just on different subjects!
WILL ROGERS

Teach your child that *there are no dumb questions!* In fact, asking questions is a sign of intelligence. The higher a student's IQ, the more likely she is to wonder and question. How kids' questions are handled at home will determine to a great extent whether she asks questions in classrooms. So handle your child's inquisitiveness with care and ask questions yourself, such as, "What are we going to do now?" "How can we solve this problem?" [7]

156

Self-confidence is a person's trust in his or her own abilities to handle situations, solve problems, deal with others effectively, and complete tasks.
**RICHARD BAUMAN,
"THE GIFT OF SELF-CONFIDENCE"**

Here are some ways to boost your child's self-confidence today:
► If you listen to his opinions and statements, he'll learn that his ideas have worth.
► Instead of shaming your child when he makes a mistake, ask, "What can you learn from this?"
► Find activities that will stretch him, make him think, and use all his mental and physical abilities. Praise him for trying!

157

*It is better to live in the corner of an attic
than with a crabby woman in a lovely home.*
PROVERBS 21:9 (TLB)

What adjustments can you make in your home
and heart so that family members feel that home is
a refuge? Here are suggestions to try today:
► Play tapes or CD's of soothing classical or
Christian music as a background.
► When possible, plan the dinner menu in the
morning or do "Once a Month" cooking so that you
can just take a meal from the freezer and heat it up.
Make the Once-a-Month cooking day great fun for the
whole family. Put on some lively music tapes and get
everyone involved in preparation and clean-up.
► If you work in a stressful environment
and tend to bring your work burdens home, stop
by an empty lot on the way home. Picture yourself
gathering up all the tensions and problems of the day,
and dump them in that empty lot. Then ask for God's
peace and love to fill you as you drive home.

158

*He who serves his brother best
Is nearer to God than all the rest.*
JOHN RUSKIN

Tonight after dinner play charades as a family. Feature
situations that deal with helping each other and people
at school, church, work, and in your neighborhood.
Then pick one service and plan to do it soon.

159

"You only need to know three things about kids,"
an eleven-year-old told his mother. "Don't hit them too much,
don't yell at them too much, and don't do
too much for them."

☞

Ask your child the three things he thinks parents
need to know about working with kids. You may be
surprised at the answer! Ask him to draw his ideas
or dictate to you if he's too young to write.

160

One can live magnificently in this world
if one knows how to work and how to love,
to work for the person one loves
and to love one's work.
LEO TOLSTOY

Here are some ways
to help your children learn to work:
► Young children *want* to help parents, so start *early*.
Two-year-olds can sort laundry; five-year-olds can put
away toys and empty garbage; seven-year-olds can set
the table, feed and walk the dog, etc.
► Show your child how to do the job the first time.
► Don't have perfect standards or "fix" their work
for them. Just compliment them!

161

The greatest delusion is to suppose that our children will be devout Christians simply because their parents have been, or that any of them will enter into the Christian faith in any other way than through their parents' deep travail of prayer and faith.

DR. JAMES DOBSON, QUOTING HIS FATHER JAMES DOBSON, SR., "FOCUS ON THE FAMILY BULLETIN," OCTOBER 1994

Pray for your child *daily,* that he or she will come to a saving knowledge of and personal relationship with Jesus Christ; that he will grow spiritually through knowing God's Word; and that he will know that in every situation and trial he can always turn to God.

162

If you are outdoors, you can recall God at least once every minute with no effort, if you remember that beauty is the voice of God. Every flower, tree, river and lake, mountain, and sunset is God speaking. . . . So as you look at each lovely thing, keep asking, "Dear Father, what are you telling me through this, and this, and this?"

FRANK LAUBACH, *GAME WITH MINUTES*

Use stars, animals, and nature to share God's character and faithfulness with your child. For example, when you point out the birds that feed in your tree, you could remark, "Isn't God a great Creator? See how He cares for the birds. He cares so much more about you!" Or when you are at the beach you can point out that God's love for us is deeper than the ocean.

163

All kids make mistakes. The children who recover and overcome failures and reversals are those who "think smart," learn from their errors, and bounce back from their setbacks. When the ones who don't know how to handle mistakes make a big error, it triggers a chain of events: failure, self-doubt, defensiveness, and finally shutdown.
**LAWRENCE J. GREENE,
"LEARNING FROM FAILURE"**

Try this strategy for making the most of mistakes:
▶ Define the problem (a low test grade).
▶ Identify the mistake (child didn't study).
▶ Brainstorm ways to solve it or correct the mistake (start three days ahead studying notes for the test; get help from teachers, etc.).

164

Manners are the happy way of doing things.
RALPH WALDO EMERSON

Teach your child the
"happy ways of doing things" by
▶ saying *thank you* when someone helps him or gives him something;
▶ saying *please* when he needs or wants something;
▶ putting his napkin in his lap and using it at meals.

165

When we see the least happening,
God may be doing the most work.
JEANNETTE OKE,
THE FATHER OF LOVE

When you pray for your teen, adult child, husband,
or friend and you don't see any changes, God is still
working unseen, and you can thank Him for His
faithful work in their lives even when nothing seems
to be happening. Meditate on James 5:16.

166

The best way to make a friend
is to be a friend.

Stock up on greeting cards:
family and friends' birthdays, sympathy cards, get-well
cards, anniversaries, new baby arrivals, and thank-you
cards. Then you can respond quickly and thoughtfully
to any situation without the stress of a trip
to the card store.

167

Wherever God has put you, that is your vocation.
It is not what we do, but how much love we put into it.
MOTHER TERESA,
"I'VE FOUND GOD"

Where has God put you at this season of your life?
If you're a wife and mother, embrace that calling
and put your heart and love into it. If you're a single,
working mom with a full- or part-time job, put your
heart into that vocation and know that God has
enough love and grace for you!

168

Before a child can say kindness, he can understand the
forgiving smile on his mother's face; before he can spell God,
he can sense his mother's anxiety dissipate as she talks
to Someone he cannot even see. Before he can understand
the concept of love, he can snuggle near his mother's heart,
closed in tight to the solid security of belonging.
JILL BRISCOE

What messages do your facial expressions
give your child? What does your child know
of your relationship to God? Does your child have
opportunities to feel that sense of belonging
by curling up on your lap?
Give him a chance today.

169

Only the open gate can receive visitors.
Only the open hand can receive gifts.
Only the open mind can receive wisdom.
Only the open heart can receive love.
JOAN WALSH ANGLUND,
THE CIRCLE OF THE SPIRIT

Invite someone new to dinner;
read a book on a subject you've never explored.
Open your heart a little wider today!

170

Scientists failed their way to success—Edison tried hundreds
of times before developing the light bulb; Salk failed countless
times before finding the polio vaccine. Failure can
point you to success.

Coach your child through failures so he learns
to be motivated and not devastated by them. Whether
it's a failing test grade when he really did study, or he
didn't make the classic soccer team, assure him he is
a loved, worthwhile member of the family; that you
are proud of his effort and there will be other contests
and other tests.

171

*Parents who allow their preschool children
to watch a lot of TV run the risk of raising children
who will learn to read later and read less.*
UNIVERSITY OF KANSAS STUDY[8]

Limit your preschooler's television watching time to
thirty minutes a day and involve her in pretend play,
building and making, listening to stories and books
read aloud, talking, outdoor play, and helping.

172

*When children are fighting among themselves,
the Lord wants them to come to peace and harmony
through His grace, not just our threats.*
**RONDA CHERVIN,
PRAYER EXERCISES FOR MOTHERS**

Try taking aside the child who is angry with his sibling
and saying, "Matt, you know your sister Ashley really
loves you. Remember how she helped you fix your
bike; remember how much fun you have together?
Jesus wants you to make up so you can
have fun again."

173

*A promise should be given with caution
and kept with care.*

Think it over before you promise your child
an activity or reward—can you deliver? Then keep
your promises, even if it's inconvenient, and you will
build in them a strong sense of trust.

174

*The character and history of each child
may be a new and poetic experience to the mother,
if she will let it.*
MARGARET FULLER

Chronicle your child's growing up years
by keeping a photojournal. Each year at birthday time,
write a letter to your child: describe character qualities
you see developing, highlights of his school year,
sports and academic accomplishments, spiritual
growth, Bible verses learned, and some of his or her
favorite sayings at that age. Put this along with photos
in an album. On his eighteenth birthday, present the
collection. What a treasure both of you will have!

175

What is this strange compulsion to go home again?
The place you were so anxious to leave, yet can never leave
altogether. Too much of you is rooted there. You thought that
you were tearing yourself away . . . yet fragments
always remain tenaciously.
MARJORIE HOLMES,
TO HELP YOU THROUGH THE HURTING

When you're sad about your child's graduation from
high school and departure for college, remember that
he'll come back! The first summer after college can be
a little rocky. Here's how to smooth it out:
▸ Talk together and set up some guidelines on
important daily issues (laundry, hours, etc.).
▸ Try to meet in the middle occasionally
for a meal and togetherness.
▸ Be patient when you see changes in your child
you didn't "order." Accept and love him.
▸ Be spontaneous and make some memories.
The summer will fly!

176

God is always faithful, and sometimes we notice.
CONNIE BAKER,
FROM AN INTERVIEW

Instead of waiting for God to do the "big things,"
recognize how His continued presence in our lives
makes a difference every day. Thank Him
with a childlike kind of gratefulness
and watch your joy grow!

177

Apathy is the glove into which evil slips its hand.
BODIE THOENE,
MUNICH SIGNATURE

Since schools decline without parent involvement,
be involved instead of apathetic:
▶ Talk to the people running for school board
and be sure to vote.
▶ Find out the "outcomes" or objectives
that steer the curriculum at each level.
▶ Offer your skills on a textbook or school
improvement committee, in the computer lab,
or on the PTA Board.

178

*Nothing is so central for a child's happiness
and sense of worth as the love of father and mother
for each other. There is no better way of giving the child
a sense of significance than to allow him to see and to feel
the closeness and commitment of his mother and father.*
JOHN DRESCHER,
SEVEN THINGS CHILDREN NEED

No matter how much you feel you can't leave your
children with anyone else, do your kids (and you
and your husband) a favor: Go out once a week
on a date—for a movie, uninterrupted conversation,
or just a serendipity evening.

179

The history of every country begins
in the heart of a man or a woman.
WILLA CATHER, O PIONEERS!

Check out biographies of great women and men
from the library and read a chapter aloud to your child
each night. Discuss what makes these people great,
admirable, and how they contributed to the
development of our country.

180

LIFE IS DIFFICULT. . . . This is a great truth,
one of the greatest truths . . . because once we truly see
this truth, we transcend it. Once we truly know that life
is difficult—once we truly understand and accept it—then
life is no longer difficult. Because once it has been accepted,
the fact that life is difficult no longer matters.
M. SCOTT PECK,
THE ROAD LESS TRAVELED

Instead of moaning about the enormity of your
problems, reflect on this truth, share it with your
children, and together memorize James 1:2-4 and John
16:33. At the dinner table, discuss the different ways
each of you has found life difficult and how God uses
those difficulties to help us mature.

181

Most people spend five years of their lives waiting in lines and six months sitting at traffic lights. We wait in doctors' offices, carpool lines, grocery store lines; we wait for children to get out of piano, sports, or dance lessons.[9]

Take resources along in a "Wait Basket"
for the times you're stuck waiting:
▶ Stationery or thank-you notes
▶ A paperback book
▶ Knitting, cross-stitch, or needlepoint
▶ A list of people for whom you want to pray

182

Most people say their families are important, but they don't live that way. The average married couple spends four minutes a day in meaningful conversation, and the working couple spends thirty seconds a day talking with their children.
MICHAEL FORTINO,
PRIORITY MANAGEMENT STUDY

No matter how busy things get, schedule regular times with your family and keep them just as if they were appointments with a major corporate executive.

183

*Certainly if we are parents we shall often need
to correct our child with firmness, but none of this is to be
from selfish motives, but only out of love for the other and a
longing for his good. Our own convenience and rights must
all the time be yielded (to God). Only so will the love of the
Lord Jesus be able to fill us and express itself through us.*

**ROY HESSION,
THE CALVARY ROAD**

When your child misbehaves, take a moment
to examine your own heart before you discipline him.
Offer yourself up to God as a vessel of love before you
give correction. Is the correction out of love
or irritability? Is your child's misbehavior
disobedience or childish action?

184

*We need to teach our kids to dream
with their eyes open.*

Have a dream-sharing time as a family.
Have each person take turns verbalizing his or her
dreams for the future: "What I want to be when I grow
up" dreams; what each person wants out of life—
travel, adventure, a big family? What can you see
yourself doing in ten or twenty years?

185

As my three children and I were memorizing verses,
my five-year-old had a precious perception of Psalm 46:1 (NIV),
which says, "God is our refuge and strength, an ever-present
help in trouble." As she tried to commit it to memory she said,
"God is our refuge and strength, a very helpful present in
trouble." We all smiled as we realized that would work! God is
like a gift, especially in difficult times, giving us such a needed
help. God is a very helpful present with a bow on top!
GAY FOWLER, FROM AN INTERVIEW

It's hard to memorize Scripture you don't understand.
So discuss the verses *first,* clarifying unfamiliar words.
Then use a big erasable board to try this fun
memorizing method: Write the verse on the board
with a bright-colored marker. Have your child say the
verse aloud and try to picture the words in his mind's
movie screen. Erase one or two words and have him
repeat the verse. Keep repeating and erasing another
word until all the words are gone. Then have your
child say the verse in its entirety, and talk about
what it means to him.

186

Shout with joy before the Lord. . . .
Obey him gladly;
come before him, singing with joy.
PSALM 100:1-2 (TLB)

Have a family music evening. Dust off your old guitar,
piano, or saxophone, get out a hymnbook or praise
song book, hand out the tambourine and kazoo,
and sing favorite songs of thanks, praise, and worship!

187

Whether we realize it or not, we're always making memories for our children. Will they remember us always rushed or upset? Or will their memories be of a mom who was full of love and had enough time to listen? Memories pile on top of each other to form a vivid image that will be recorded forever on a child's heart.

Reflect on the memories you have of home and family and what memories you hope to leave with your children. Make a warm, loving memory today.

188

Often we have no idea where our children or spouse are in their relationships with God. We may assume they're experiencing the same level of intimacy with Him that we are. Yet we must stay sensitive to the fact that they might be going through a spiritual struggle we need to pray for.

Gather your family, sit in a circle on the floor, and give each person a piece of paper and a pencil or marker. Ask each family member to draw a picture that best describes their present relationship with God. Go around the circle and let each explain his or her picture.

189

My little Donny, while riding on my lap in the front seat
of the car said to me, "Mommy, when I grow up I'm going
to marry you." "Oh, honey, you can't do that. I'm already
married." "You are?" he asked. Twenty years flew by. He
married someone else. We have those moments
for such a short time.

THELMA AVORE,
FROM AN INTERVIEW

Hold your child's hand or let him sit on your lap
whenever you can. It won't be long before he won't let
you or he will be too big!

190

Busy hands are happy hands.
MILDRED MORRISON HEATH (MY MOM)

As a mother of six, my mom found this philosophy
very practical. It's worked for me as well. Provide your
kids their own "Activity Table" nearby that contains
drawing paper, markers, gluestick, collage materials
(dried beans, different shaped pasta, sequins, buttons,
etc.), clay, cardboard to make board games, and other
items for making their own fun while you cook or do
other work. You can transfer these items to a lap
container for keeping hands busy on car trips.

191

*Some of the best opportunities you'll ever have
to educate your children—develop values and strengthen
their faith—will occur at the dinner table.
It's the perfect "conversation college."*

Use mealtime for conversations about world events,
community, school, church, and what you believe
and feel about issues. Whether your "table-talk" time is
at breakfast, lunch, or dinner,
► unplug the phone;
► keep it pleasant;
► ask your children's opinions;
► make schedule adjustments so that you have
at least thirty minutes together.

192

*Kids seem to need the most love
when they are the most unlovable.*

Which child are you having the most trouble with this
week? Commit to spending at least fifteen minutes
with that child *each day* doing something simple she
would enjoy. This method has transformed many
children's behavior within three to four weeks!

193

The taproot of reality in the Christian family
is the recognition of the sacred meaning of each person.
Out of this realization comes the flowering of respect
for one another that makes familial love so fragrant.
HAZEN G. WERNER,
CHRISTIAN FAMILY LIVING

For your child's next birthday, celebrate her as a gift
of God. Two weeks before the birthday, start working
on a memory book of photos and mementos. Siblings
or parents can write poems or little stories that show
the qualities they love best about the child. On the
special day, along with a meal of favorite food and
cake, present the memory book and have each person
pray a special blessing for the birthday child.

194

The persons who are hardest to convince
they're at the retirement age are children at bedtime.
SHANNON FIFE

Make bedtime a special part of the day by taking a few
minutes to read aloud to your child. Or give him a
little back rub while listening to the details of his day,
and pray with him. Bedtime routine can mean a world
of security to a child.

195

*Any reasonable person might think that once through this
curious drama of love were enough [i.e., the pregnancy and
delivery of a child]. Once to labor at making room; once to
labor at emptying it. But the mother is asked to do it all over
again. . . . Then, for the second time, comes the second
suffering. At the child's maturity, she must birth him
not out of her body, but out of her house
and into the world, an independent being.*

WALTER WANGERIN, JR.,
RAGMAN AND OTHER CRIES OF FAITH

When your child graduates from high school or goes
to college, or whatever form that first independent
journey takes, allow yourself time to cry, to reflect on
memories and talk with close friends about your
feelings. This will help move you through
the inevitable "letting go."

196

Death and life are in the power of the tongue.
PROVERBS 18:21 (NASB)

Notice the words you speak to your children each day.
Do they bring *life* (build up confidence and a sense
of being loved), or *death* (tear down self-esteem and
verbally injure)? Let your children know you believe
in them and think the best of them.

197

*All great teachers know that asking questions
is one of the best teaching strategies. And no one was better
at asking questions than Jesus. Check the four gospels
in the New Testament and count the many questions!*

Try engaging your children's minds by asking them
questions instead of always telling them what to do.
Ask: What's the most important thing for you to get
accomplished today? What is the real issue here and
what are the facts? How can we solve this problem?

198

*To any parent who is interested in homeschooling,
my advice is: Give it a try. You don't have to make a 12-year
commitment. You don't have to have a Ph.D. to be a good
teacher. If you have a "love of learning," it could be the most
rewarding experience of your life.*
**MICKI COLFAX,
"FROM HOMESCHOOLING TO HARVARD"**

Read the Colfax family's book, *Homeschooling for
Excellence*, to find out more about their experiment
in homeschooling that led to their sons' acceptance
and education at Harvard and Yale. Go to a local
homeschool association meeting and talk with other
parents who have experienced that schooling choice.

199

The only certainty is uncertainty;
the only constant is change.

How do you handle change—moving to a different
city, a daughter's sudden spurt into adolescence, a son's
departure for college? Since change continually
impacts our lives as mothers, I have prayed for years,
"Lord, guide me through the transitions that are yet to
come." Remember that no matter what losses change
brings, God has gains in store for you too, and in Him,
the gains always outweigh the losses.

200

Out of the presses of pain
Cometh the soul's best wine
And the eyes that have shed no rain
Can shed but little shine.
PAUL BILLHEIMER,
DON'T WASTE YOUR SORROWS

Paul Billheimer suggests that when sorrow
and suffering come, instead of giving in to self-pity
and resentment, we offer our suffering to God
that He might use it to bless others
and reflect His glory even more.

201

Who are your child's major relationships? Are they with the television or with her parents? If a parent is spending a few minutes a day with his or her child in actual conversation, and the child is watching five to six hours of television a day, the TV will constitute a pretty powerful influence.

**DR. ERIC DLUGOKINSKI,
"LIMITING AMOUNT OF TV TIME FOR CHILDREN"**

Try an "Unplug the TV week" in your home. Substitute a different activity each evening: One night put together a big puzzle; the next, cook hamburgers and marshmallows outside and watch the stars; read a mystery aloud; play games all evening, and so on.

202

Playing games is a good way to exercise the memory and develop problem-solving skills that will serve your child in both the classroom and in life. At the same time, the child has fun and enjoys social interaction.

As often as possible, get out the board games and play with your children. Short games work best for younger children; simple games such as *Tic Tac Toe, Old Maid,* and *Chutes and Ladders* are good if there are several children.

203

Life is all memory, except for the one present moment
that goes by you so quick you hardly catch it going.
TENNESSEE WILLIAMS

Throughout your child's school career,
save report cards, school photos, friends' photos,
newspaper clippings, programs from special events,
sports and academic awards, college acceptance letter,
etc., and put them in a scrapbook to give your child
on graduation day.

204

Diverse children have their different natures:
some are like flesh which nothing but salt will keep from
putrefaction, some again like tender fruits that are best
preserved with sugar. Those parents are wise that can fit their
nurture according to their children's natures.
ANNE BRADSTREET,
"MEDITATIONS DIVINE AND MORAL"

Think about the unique discipline dilemmas you face
with each of your children. One discipline does not fit
all! Which child needs a sensitive, gentle approach
("sugar")? Which child responds to verbal correction?
Which one needs firmer discipline ("salt")? Work
on giving each child what he or she needs.

205

"What's it like to raise a teenager?" a parent once asked me.
"Well," I replied, "do you remember what your toddler was
like when he went through the Terrible Twos stage?
Just multiply that by eight and add a driver's license!"
LIZ TARPY

Although parenting teenagers is a challenge,
it can also be great fun if we occasionally take time to
meet them on their own turf. Take your teen out (or
better yet, let her drive you!) for a hamburger; shoot
a few hoops; go to an art museum. The main thing is
to enjoy time together and talk about whatever
is on your teen's mind.

206

Children live in the present, and they know when we are with
them physically but not mentally. By worrying about the past
and future, we lose the present and our children
don't have us, even when we are around.
DAVID ELKIND,
THE HURRIED CHILD

Take a little time *today* to watch the sunset with your
child, fly a kite, or play with new kittens. If you're a
working mom, don't worry about the time you weren't
there or when you'll be away from your child
tomorrow. Enjoy being together now.

207

*Creativity is a God-given ability to take something ordinary
and make it into something special. It is an openness to doing
old things in new ways. . . . The creative spirit is part of our
heritage as children of the One who created all things.
And nurturing our creativity is part of our responsibility
as stewards of God's good gifts.*

**EMILIE BARNES,
THE SPIRIT OF LOVELINESS**

Nurture your creativity and replenish it if you feel it's
depleted. Here are a couple of suggestions:
▶ Take a class or try a hobby you've
always wanted to do.
▶ Get a change of scenery;
walk along a lake or nature center.

208

*If you're always thinking you'll be happy when you lose those
twenty pounds or when your child gets potty-trained or when
you and your spouse solve your financial problems, that day
may never come. Don't miss out on joy now!*

Write this verse on an index card or embroider or
cross-stitch it as a reminder to rejoice *today and every
day*: "This is the day the Lord has made. I will rejoice
and be glad in it."

209

The steady rhythm of a rocking chair eases stress much as exercise does. Rocking soothes restless babies and relaxes elderly adults.

Rock away some tension today. Read and rock for a short while, or even better, rock your child and sing to him.

210

Just as love to God begins with listening to His Word, so the beginning of love for the brethren is learning to listen to them. It is God's love for us that He not only gives us His Word but also lends us His ear. So it is His work that we do for our brother when we learn to listen to Him. . . . Listening can be a greater service than speaking.

**DIETRICH BONHOEFFER,
LIFE TOGETHER**

When your child wants to talk, tune in. Don't try to control the conversation and get your "two cents" in; think carefully before you respond to what he has said.

211

Preparation helps to dispel fear.

Verbal cues reduce a child's anxiety. Preparing your child for the immediate future decreases conflicts and increases cooperation. For example, telling your child "The McCoys are coming over for dinner tonight," or "In twenty minutes we leave for the school program; soon you can start putting away your paints and washing your brushes" gives him a sense of control over what's going to happen next.

212

If I could begin my family again, I would seek to share God more intimately with my children. By this I mean I would seek, like Christ himself, to choose the ordinary and special things of every day to illustrate the God who loves us.
JOHN DRESCHER,
IF I WERE STARTING MY FAMILY AGAIN

Point out to your children as you go about your lives the "ordinary and special things of each day." Let them know that God has provided food, animals, sunsets, the varied colors of flowers, the songs of birds, nighttime to sleep . . . the list is endless. Encourage them to add to the list!

213

Children are the freest and most imaginative of creatures. They love the fun of words and have a spectacular ability to learn.

GLADYS HUNT,
HONEY FOR A CHILD'S HEART

Increase your child's imagination, awareness, and word power by making a game of asking questions such as, What does it feel like to be soaked from a sudden rain? How do you think a space shuttle looks when it's about to take off? Ask each child to answer in whatever detail she can. Compliment rather than criticize her answer.

214

Before most people start boasting about their family tree, they usually do a good pruning job.

O. A. BATTISTA

Instead of pruning off all the undesirables from your family tree, share stories with your child about the "black sheep" in the family and what you can learn from his or her life. Tell them, too, about the rebel, the family clown, and the late bloomer who surprised everyone and made their lives count.

215

Like the perennial flower that blooms once a year to give us joy, the traditions we share together remind us of who we are and where we have been as a family.

Make Family Memory Ornaments: Cut thin plywood circles about three to four inches in diameter. Drill a tiny hole in the top for hangers. Paint the front and back with white acrylic paint. When dry, let the family artists sketch a picture memory—scenes from the year such as a family wedding or vacation—and then color it in with fine-tip colored markers or paints. On the back, date the ornaments, put decorative cord through the holes, and hang them on the tree. You can enjoy your family memories year after year and add more each year.

216

Giving happiness brings happiness.

Who can you give a little happiness to today? Think about someone and what makes him or her happy. (A little vase with a single rose? A plate of hot apple muffins?) Do it today!

217

What you see is mainly what you look for.

Look for the best in your kids! Jot down what each child excels in—what comes naturally, what he does better than others, or what he wants to know more about. Beside the area of talent listed, write one way you could help develop that skill in your child and move him closer to mastery of it.

218

One way to cultivate a taste for Christian music in your children is through sharing a testimony song. This is a song that expresses your love for God and describes your walk with the Lord. . . . It lets someone else understand why you love Jesus. Every Christian should have a testimony song.

AL MENCONI,
TODAY'S MUSIC

Ask your child for five minutes of her time. Show her a song that means a lot to you and have her read the lyrics while you play the song. Then ask to listen to a song that has meaning to her.

219

Take the possibility, the diagnosis [about your special needs child] and lay it at the feet of Christ. Listen for His direction—what He guides you to do for your child— and it will make all the difference in the world.

PAM WHITELY,
FROM AN INTERVIEW

If you are the parent of a special needs child, you may be given many negative reports about your child from professionals. View the report as a possibility, but look to God as the final authority.

220

A mind is a terrible thing to waste!
ADVERTISEMENT FOR THE NEGRO COLLEGE FUND

Stretch your child's mind by asking and encouraging challenging and fun questions; you can collect questions from the newspaper, magazines, and other sources. Here's an example of a "mind-stretcher": Which three states have the highest percentage of people who play golf? Answer: Minnesota, Wisconsin, North Dakota.

221

One important value I've endeavored to pass on to my children is to enjoy being in nature and to appreciate what God has given us—to be aware that we can see His very nature in the things He has created.

CANDY MATHENY,
FROM AN INTERVIEW

Mark off a small (typing paper size to poster-board size) plot of ground at a park or forest near your home. Put small stakes (wooden popsicles sticks) at the edge of the plot and return every six weeks all year long to observe it. Have your children discuss how things have changed in that particular plot of ground.

222

Where Mercy, Love, and Pity dwell
There God is dwelling too.

WILLIAM BLAKE,
"THE DIVINE IMAGE"

Any time you and your family pass or observe an auto accident, pray together for the individuals involved and you will see your children develop mercy and compassion instead of growing callous to the suffering around them.

223

When one of my kids asks, "When's the character training going to be over?" I have to tell them it's still going on with me and it's still going on with their grandma (who is past seventy), and I guess it's not going to get over until we see Jesus and are like Him.
KAREN COLLE,
FROM AN INTERVIEW

When your children have a bad situation to deal with in sports or school, pray with them and *ask God to build their character through it.* Pray for the character qualities of Jesus to grow in your children and share with them how God is working in your character.

224

Pretend play is not a waste of time; in fact, it is essential to children's growth and learning. It encourages creativity, language development, communication skills, and helps kids realize the symbol system which undergirds understanding words as symbols (reading) and numbers as symbols (math).
DR. DOROTHY LOEFFLER,
FROM AN INTERVIEW

Encourage your children's pretend play by
▶ providing them with costumes, props, hats, and puppets (garage sales, second-hand stores, and attics are good places to find such items);
▶ giving them enough *time* to play in an unhurried atmosphere with siblings, friends, and by themselves.

225

God does not comfort us to make us comfortable,
but to make us comforters.
J. H. JOWLETT

To comfort means to lift the spirits of someone,
to give strength, cheer, and hope. Plan a way to give
comfort today to someone in your child's world:
a teacher just out of the hospital; a child alone
every day after school.

226

New studies show that during the school years it is what
parents do at home, more than any other factor, that makes
the difference between success or failure for their children.[10]

Is your home a supportive environment for your
child's learning and successful development? Are there
predictable times for family meals, homework, and
bedtime? Is there much encouragement to read? Do
you keep in touch with your child's teachers? Any
time you spend with your child in a learning activity,
however simple, will multiply back to you as his
motivation grows.

227

One of the most powerful things you can do to enhance and strengthen your child's education is to let her see you enjoying your own curiosity, expanding your intellect, and learning from new experiences. As you love learning, your child learns to enjoy her own curiosity, intellect, creativity and talent. She becomes, in fact, a lifelong learner!

DR. CHARLES GOUAUX,
FROM AN INTERVIEW

What hobby or interest can you share with your child?

228

Teaching your child to knit is a great way to develop fine motor skills and increase focus and attention span.

My friend Margolyn Woods, who has taught many children to knit, offers these tips: Use big knitting needles (size thirteen); let your child pick out the color of an inexpensive yarn; plan on spending some time together as you *patiently show, explain, and encourage* him or her how to knit.

229

*Instead of over-reacting by burning CD's or blowing our tops
about our teenagers' rock music, let's encourage them
to know Christ in a closer relationship and point them
in the right musical direction.*

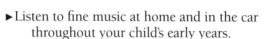

▸ Listen to fine music at home and in the car
throughout your child's early years.
▸ Set guidelines as a family for the music you listen to,
but always undergird everything you say and do
concerning it with *love and prayer.*
▸ Invest in the best Christian, folk, and classical music,
and go see the artists perform when you can.[11]

230

*It is a foolish woman who expects her husband to be
to her that which only Jesus Christ Himself can be: always
ready to forgive, totally understanding, unendingly patient,
invariably tender and loving, unfailing in every area,
anticipating every need, and making more than adequate
provision. Such expectations put a man under an impossible
strain. . . . The same goes for the man who expects
too much from his wife.*
RUTH BELL GRAHAM,
IT'S MY TURN

Write down *your* expectations of your husband and
give these to God. Then look to God's Word for
instruction on what you are to be to your spouse,
he to you, and most of all, who Christ is to you
and how He meets your needs.

231

Prayer empowers a family. It is in that vital experience of family prayer that members of a family grow in power to meet the needs that arise in the process of living together day by day.
HAZEN G. WERNER,
CHRISTIAN FAMILY LIVING

To add variety to family prayer time:
►Light a candle in the dark and pray for each other.
►Circle prayer: Each person thanks God for something in creation or a blessing he received today.
►An older child reads a psalm.

232

Marriage should, I think, always be a little hard and new and strange. It should be breaking your shell and going into another world, and a bigger one.
ANNE MORROW LINDBERGH,
QUOTED IN UNCOMMON FRIENDS

As you go through each stage of marriage— early and middle parenthood, parenting teens, empty nest, etc., be expectant about the new things you will learn about one another. You're never too old for an adventure! Always be on the lookout for new places to go or things to do with your spouse.

233

*I did not have my mother long, but she cast over me
an influence which lasted all my life. . . . If it had not been for
her appreciation and her faith in me at a critical time in my
experience, I should never likely have become an inventor.
I was always a careless boy. . . . But her firmness, her
sweetness, her goodness, were potent powers
to keep me in the right path.*
THOMAS A. EDISON

Some of a child's most challenging experiences can
bring out his greatest strengths as an adult. Show faith
in your child and in his gifts—determination,
curiosity, logic, resourcefulness, creativity. Keep
believing in him even if no one else does. You never
know; you may have another Edison in your
home when he grows into his gifts!

234

*Children are islands of curiosity
surrounded by a sea of question marks.*

When your child asks a question, show enthusiasm.
If you don't know the answer or don't have a book to
look it up, write the question on an index card (keep a
stack on the kitchen counter). Next time you and your
child are close to the library, take the question card
and discover the answer together!

235

Children in a family are like flowers in a bouquet:
there's always one determined to face in an opposite
direction from the way the arranger desires.

MARCELENE COX,
FROM AN INTERVIEW

Which of your children "faces in the opposite
direction" from the way you expected or the direction
your other children are facing? Celebrate her
differences and remember that this child may be
the one who most needs your love and affirmation.

236

If I can stop one heart from breaking
I shall not live in vain:
If I can ease one life the aching
Or cool one pain,
Or help one fainting robin
Unto his nest again,
I shall not live in vain.

EMILY DICKINSON,
SELECTED POEMS AND LETTERS OF EMILY DICKINSON

Teaching your children to memorize poetry not only
fills their minds with good values, it gives them
models of fine expression and improves their
memories. Start with this one!

237

Slow down is my best advice to young mothers.
We can get so involved with doing things and getting
everything done that we begin to look at our children
as interruptions instead of our priorities!
LEONETTE GRAY,
FROM AN INTERVIEW

Today, take some slow-down time with your child
to read a story (slowly) or just to have
tea and cookies and chat.

238

All altars are not confined to churches. Your altar may be
your desk, the machine you operate, the kitchen stove.
MARJORIE HOLMES,
I'VE GOT TO TALK TO SOMEBODY, GOD

Take a prayer walk around the block. Talk to God
about each of your children, your husband, and your
own concerns. Continue your dialogue with Him
as you walk through the rest of your day, as you work
and care for your family. Know that He can be
worshiped through any of the tasks you
commit to Him.

239

Never give up on a child in sin.
Instead of giving up hope, ask God to
▶ *give her a hunger for righteousness;*
▶ *take the blinders off so she will see*
the deceptions of Satan;
▶ *flood her with friends who will influence her*
positively for Him.

CAROL HARRISON,
FROM AN INTERVIEW

240

We earn the right to be heard by our adolescents by showing
interest in them, giving them time, and listening to them.

LINDA SIMONSEN,
FROM AN INTERVIEW

Besides being available on a day-to-day basis for your
teen, set aside nonthreatening, pleasant times for
talking such as Saturday breakfast out or riding along
with you on an errand and stopping for a soda
afterward.

241

Rules are only as good as our willingness to follow them ourselves. We can't teach children to respect privacy if we open their mail or burst into their rooms. We can't get them to be honest if we lower their age to get a ticket discount.
BARBARA SOFER, "HOW TO RAISE MORAL KIDS IN AN IMMORAL WORLD"

What are your rules for living? Are you following them? If you slip up and violate them, don't hesitate to admit it to your child—"I shouldn't have pulled in front of that car when it wasn't my turn. . . ."

242

The mystery of language was revealed to me. I knew then that "w-a-t-e-r" meant the wonderful cool something that was flowing over my hand. That living word awakened my soul, gave it light, joy, and set it free!
HELEN KELLER, THE STORY OF MY LIFE

Awaken your child's understanding of language by making sure she learns to read well. No matter what handicap or problem, almost every person can learn to read with the right method. Find that method and don't accept a "reading disabled" label. That's a sure sentence to low self-esteem and failure.

243

The road to a friend's house is never long.
DANISH PROVERB

Invite a friend over for lunch today. Even a sandwich
with tomato soup can be a special time of fellowship.

244

Let family worship be short, savory,
simple, plain, tender, heavenly.
RICHARD CECIL

Buy a worship tape to play while you sing
and give praise together during family devotions.
Take turns reading God's promises that reassure His
love and comfort for the present situations family
members may be facing.

245

What a commentary on civilization, when being alone is
considered suspect; when one has to apologize for it, make
excuses, hide the fact that one practices it—like a secret vice.
ANNE MORROW LINDBERGH

Allow your child or teen "alone-time" in his or her
room; give him the privacy of knowing a knock will
precede visitors into his space. Also, give yourself
permission to have time alone and enjoy it.

246

*When teenagers are pulling away and pushing the limits,
often the parent pulls away or distances herself. But it is
important for parents not to pull away or sever the
relationship! Adolescents are not ready for complete
emotional or financial independence.*

*Picture your parent-teen relationship like two people
at the end of a rope, each tugging. If you keep tugging and he
does, you get closer to the middle. If you let go of the rope, he
falls down and is headed for trouble. Worse, the teen ends up
feeling "My parents don't care about me."*

Keep holding your end of the rope!

ADELE FABER

247

*When you nurture your children's awareness
of others' needs and feelings, you help them develop
kindness and a caring attitude.*

Help your child think about someone else's point
of view by asking, *"How would you feel if . . . ?"* Your
child might say, "I don't want to go to Sally's party.
Nobody likes her." You could respond, "How would
you feel if we prepared a birthday party for you
and no one came . . . ?"

248

If you can't sleep, don't count sheep . . .
Talk to the Shepherd.
RUTHANN WINANS,
FROM AN INTERVIEW

When something is keeping you up at night, turn it
into a prayer instead of holding onto it as a burden.
Writing out your prayer on a restless night
and reading the Psalms can be soothing.

249

The warmth of a home is not necessarily determined
by its heating system.

Increase the warmth in your home by
➤ more hugs and physical affection;
➤ more praise and positive comments;
➤ more prayer and laughter.

250

What do girls do who haven't any mothers
to help them through their troubles?
LOUISA MAY ALCOTT

Sometimes the most comfort we can offer our
daughters when they are sad or in turmoil is not
advice but understanding and unconditional love. The
next time your daughter is upset, try quiet empathy,
especially until you've heard her out.

251

We are sometimes tempted to think that the Lord does not hear our prayers. But let the mother teach us. Could she possibly let the cry of her child go unheeded? Is the earthly mother more tender than the heavenly Father?

HANNAH WHITALL SMITH,
GOD IS ENOUGH

Think about your attentiveness to your child when he is suffering and how you care for him when he is sick. Remember that God does not close His ear to us when we are struggling through dark days, but He is nearest to our cry at those times. Draw close to His everlasting arms today!

252

I am sure it is a great mistake always to know enough to go in when it rains. One may keep snug and dry by such knowledge, but one misses a world of loveliness.

ADELINE KNAPP,
READER'S DIGEST

Whatever the weather or season today, get out for a short while and enjoy the world of loveliness around your home! Bundle up or take an umbrella if needed, take your dog on a leash, and invite your kids or a neighbor.

253

It is the greatest of all mistakes to do nothing because you can only do little—Do what you can.

At your child's school, do the *one thing* that you can. If your skill is gardening, offer to plant bulbs or flowers around it. If it's writing, help the children write and "publish" their own books. If you like to lead, serve on a textbook committee or the PTA. One of the best ways of making a difference is building a relationship with a teacher.

254

Play is often talked about as if it were a relief from serious learning. But for children, play is serious learning. Play is really the work of childhood.
MR. FRED ROGERS,
"YOU ARE SPECIAL"

Provide a big box from which your child can make a playhouse, fort, or "hideout." Then make sure he has some blocks of unstructured time just to play.

255

*The Spirit of Christ is the spirit of missions,
and the nearer we get to Him, the more intensely
missionary we must become.*
HENRY MARTYN

Develop a heart for missions in your family:
- ▶ Have a missionary on furlough to dinner
at your home.
- ▶ Read your children a missionary story each day
at breakfast or lunch; even preschoolers can be
fascinated by faith adventures.
- ▶ Find the country you are discussing on a world map
and pray for the people of that country.

256

*Grandparents can build relationships in the institution
most vital to the future of children today—the family.
They can strengthen the bonds of love and provide
a strong sense of security to their grandchildren.*
**MARGOLYN WOODS,
GRANDMA'S LITTLE ACTIVITY BOOK**

Plan a picnic and invite the grandparents.
If they live far away, ask Grandma to write a letter to
your child, perhaps sending a picture or stickers with
instructions to *write back*! Then encourage your child
to answer promptly.

257

*God asks us to do our part in loving our children
unconditionally, teaching them the Word of God,
and taking them to church. As a mom, I've had to learn
to leave the impossible parts to God—I can't change their
hearts or give them right thinking or make them
love Jesus. That's the Holy Spirit's part.*

FERN NICHOLS,
FROM AN INTERVIEW

Of the three "possible" parts Fern mentions for a mom
to do, which one could you put into action today?

258

*We rush kids to school, lessons, sports practice,
church activities, to finish homework . . . and then
are surprised when they get burned out, exhausted,
and develop stress disorders.*

Let each of your children choose one sport,
regular activity, or lesson he or she really wants to
pursue each semester. Once the activity is started,
consider it a commitment until the end of the term,
and then another activity can be chosen
or the same one continued.

259

*Since my mom taught me it was more blessed to give
than receive, I thought, What can I give of myself
to Kyser [my son] each Christmas? I wanted to give him
the opportunity to hear and tell stories, to know his own
history, and to treasure mementos that might be discarded
as he grows up. Most of all, I was trying to teach him
to give to others.*
POSY LOUGH

Make a Storytelling Stocking: Sew twenty-four
tiny ribbons on the front side of the stocking. Collect
twenty-four mementos of your child's life so far and
put them inside the stocking (a bootie knitted by
Grandma, his hospital bracelet, etc.). Each day during
Advent he can take out one object; you tie it to
a ribbon and tell him the story of that memento.
Change the mementos each year as he grows
and have him begin telling the story
behind the treasure as soon as he can.

260

Parents are the bones on which children cut their teeth.
PETER USTINOV

Be as patient with your teenagers as they find their
identities—trying out hairstyles, clothes, and fads—
as you were when they were cutting their first teeth!

261

Keeping curiosity alive is critical to motivation.
It's the ingredient that carries a child's learning far beyond
the three R's and makes him a lifelong learner.

Is there anything *you* are curious about or want to
know more about? Investigate it and discuss it with
your children. Appreciate their sense of curiosity
whenever you can instead of squelching it. Delight
in the myriad questions young people ask.

262

A good, warm friendship is like a good, warm fire.
You need to keep stoking it.
DEE BRESTIN, "WOMEN AND FRIENDSHIP"
FOCUS ON THE FAMILY BROADCAST

Cultivate your friendship with another woman by
sending an encouraging note, taking her a loaf of
blueberry bread, or calling to see how her family is.

263

Marriage turns out to be a mirror.
Each reflects the other, which is bound to be
in some degree painful, for none of us
can bear too much reality at once.
ELISABETH ELLIOT,
LET ME BE A WOMAN

Examine the characteristics in your husband
that most irritate you. How do these qualities
reflect or bring out your own shortcomings?

264

If in dealing with one who does not respond,
I weary of the strain, and slip from under the burden,
then I know nothing of Calvary love.
AMY CARMICHAEL, IF

Is there someone you've helped or loved
who is not responding to your overtures? Is one of
your children not responding in obedience or failing
to live up to your expectations? Let Christ help you
carry the burden. Pray for the person, and ask for
the grace to keep loving him or her.

265

*The first hour in the morning
is the rudder of the day.*
HENRY WARD BEECHER

Wake up your family with a song.
Marching music peps everyone up. Blend an "energy
drink" with fruit, yogurt, protein powder, and ice
cubes to accompany breakfast and start the day
with enough nutrition to carry you through.

266

*If you want children to keep their feet on the ground,
put some responsibility on their shoulders.*
**ABIGAIL VAN BUREN,
UNITED PRESS SYNDICATE**

Build responsibility in adolescents by asking them
to do for themselves what you've been doing for them:
laundry, paying car insurance, making
their own expense money.

267

*Children are the living messages we send
to a time we will not see.*
JOHN WHITEHEAD,
THE STEALING OF AMERICA

Keep family traditions throughout the year, such as
reading the Christmas story from the Bible; making a
special cake for birthdays with a note signed by each
family member expressing appreciation for the
birthday person; decorating the Christmas tree the day
after Thanksgiving. Traditions not only pass on
important values and beliefs to your child, they also tie
your family together from generation to generation.

268

*A friend told me one day that I needed to lose weight.
I went out and ate three chocolate bars. I know my bad
points probably better than anybody else, and didn't need her
harping on what's wrong with me. God showed me that my
children react the same way. The more I talk about
something I don't like in them, the worse it gets.*
KAREN COLLE,
FROM AN INTERVIEW

What don't you like in your child? Messiness?
Laziness? Instead of nagging him about it, pray for the
opposite positive quality to grow in your child—
orderliness, diligence, etc. Then major on their good
qualities, not their faults.

269

*If I were given the opportunity to present a gift
to the next generation, it would be the ability for each
individual to learn to laugh at himself.*
CHARLES SCHULTZ

Give your children the gift of laughing at themselves
by telling them humorous stories about small or large
mistakes you have made.

270

*Trying to educate children without their parents' involvement
is like playing basketball with only four players on the court.*

Be involved by
►attending parent-teacher conferences;
►discussing with your child's teachers education
objectives and how you can support
your child at home;
►sharing your expertise with the school.

271

If children haven't been read to, they don't love books.
They need to love books, for books are the basis
of literature, composition, history, world events,
vocabulary, and everything else.
EDITH SCHAEFFER

Since many schools often give mediocre reading
assignments, which are the literary equivalent of junk
food, supplement your child's reading at home. Check
the list of wonderful classics for all ages in "Can't-Miss
Treasures" section of my book *Helping Your Child
Succeed in Public School* (or write P. O. Box 770493,
Oklahoma City, OK 73177. Include an SASE).

272

There is nothing worse than being a doer
yet having nothing to do!

For the active, energetic child, find ways he or she
can constructively use all that energy. Perhaps he can
help parents or neighbors with yard work, gardening,
washing the car, or walking pets.

273

*I don't think of all the misery
but of the beauty that still remains.*
ANNE FRANK,
THE DIARY OF A YOUNG GIRL

When you get down in the dumps,
write in your journal about all the beauty around you,
the things and the people you are thankful for,
and the ways you've seen God bring beauty
out of the worst situations.

274

*Any concern too small to be turned into a prayer
is too small to be made into a burden.*
CORRIE TEN BOOM

Is there anything burdening your mind today?
Turn it into a prayer. The God who cares about
the sparrows and knows the number of hairs
on your head cares about your concerns.

275

By looking at them [the older women] the younger women
will know how to love their husbands and children,
be virtuous and pure, keep a good house, be good wives.
TITUS 2:3-5 (*THE MESSAGE*)

Find an "older woman," a woman farther along
in the mothering journey than you are, and ask her to
spend time with you as a mentor, encouraging you to
be a godly wife and mother and sharing her wisdom
and experience with you. If you know of a younger
mother who needs such mentoring, take
the initiative to reach out to her.

276

A plant must have roots below as well as sunlight above
and roots must be grubby. Much of the grubbiness is clean
dirt if only you will leave it in the garden and not keep
sprinkling it over the library table.
C. S. LEWIS

Being accepted where you are spiritually
and emotionally is a giant growth step. Since God
accepts us and looks beyond the dirt and grime we are
all covered with, let's embrace our children as they are,
spilled milk, messy rooms, and all! When you see
some of their dirt or mistakes, don't air them in front
of your children's friends or relatives.

277

Over a period of years, with Mother's constant
encouragement, both Curtis and I started believing
that we really could do anything we chose to do. Maybe she
brainwashed us into believing we were going to be extremely
good and highly successful at whatever we attempted. Even
today I can clearly hear her voice in the back of my head
saying, "Bennie, you can do it. Don't you stop believing that
for one second," "You weren't born to be a failure, Bennie,"
or one of her favorites, "You just ask the Lord,
and He'll help you."
BEN CARSON, M.D.,
GIFTED HANDS

Keep believing in each of your children,
no matter what their limitations or struggles.
Let your high hopes and belief in them be revealed
in the way you speak to them.

278

So many times we look at all our problems and feel
overwhelmed. We wonder how we can ever solve them all.
But if we decide to solve just one big problem a day, we will
end up with a magnificent family.
TIM HANSEL,
QUOTED IN *PARENTS AND CHILDREN*

What is one problem plaguing your family that you
could work on today? Identify it and brainstorm
solutions with your spouse, a friend, or children. Then
put the plan into action. Do one thing at a time!

279

Mothers of young children have distinct needs at this particular stage of life. They can feel isolated. They definitely have less energy and operate on less sleep and have less money. We try to address the needs of young mothers for understanding and belonging. That's how we nurture them.
ELISA MORGAN,
"MOM'S THE WORD"

Join a support group for young mothers such as MOPS (Mothers of Preschoolers) or help start one. This gives you the opportunity to get out of the house and share with others who are in the same stage of mothering. Write MOPS, 1311 South Clarkson, Denver, CO 80210 for a group in your area or to find out how to start one. You can also check out local churches about their mothers' groups.

280

Children are like flowers—they need to be watered (praised), showered with sunshine (encouraged) and rooted in love (taught God's unconditional love through the love of their parents), in order to bloom.
TAMMY LOVELL,
FROM AN INTERVIEW

Praise your children for the inward qualities you want them to develop (joy, perseverance, kindness, etc.), not just for their outward successes. Let your encouragement be steady and warm them like a summer day. Root them in God's love and trust Him to bring a bountiful harvest in their lives!

281

*Part of being highly creative is pushing ourselves
into areas in which we are at a distinct disadvantage;
areas in which the presuppositions are strange and
unfamiliar . . . areas in which we cannot rattle off
the latest statistics or make small talk with great
confidence. While this can be threatening, it is also
very life-giving. Diversity stimulates creativity.*
**RICHARD ALLEN FARMER,
IT WON'T FLY IF YOU DON'T TRY**

Purchase a book or newspaper from another city and
see what people are doing in other places. Read whole
books, short chapters, articles, paragraphs, footnotes,
and anything else you can get your hands on!
Stimulating your creativity and love for learning
is a boost to everyone in the family.

282

*Why pray for their future husbands even while our daughters
are little girls? Because somewhere in the world those future
husbands—whoever they may be—are little boys. With the
pressures to conform to this world, those little boys need a lot
of prayer. . . . Even though I don't even know who
I'm praying for, God does.*
AL MENCONI, TODAY'S MUSIC

Pray for the husband or wife of your child from today
on. Pray that God will bring this life partner into your
child's life in His perfect timing, and that Christ will be
the center of their relationship and their home.

283

As a mother, I must faithfully, patiently, lovingly,
and happily do my part—then quietly wait
for God to do His.
RUTH BELL GRAHAM,
PRODIGALS AND THOSE WHO LOVE THEM

Pray for the wisdom to know what is your part
in this season of mothering and what is God's part.
Ask for the wisdom to know the difference
and the patience to wait for Him.

284

A labor of love is never lost in heaven's eyes.

Remember that all the serving, loving, cooking,
carpooling, and caring for your children is seen and
appreciated by your heavenly Father, even if at times
no one else seems to notice.

285

Prayer is the mightiest force in the world.
FRANK LAUBACH,
CHRIST LIVETH IN ME

Tonight, discuss at the dinner table
the times God answered prayer
and really surprised and delighted you.

286

*The family should be the place where each new human being
can have an early atmosphere conducive
to the development of constructive creativity.*
**EDITH SCHAEFFER,
WHAT IS A FAMILY?**

Let a different child each week make the dinner table
centerpiece out of his or her "favorite things" or most
treasured collection. During the meal, have this child
explain the objects on the table. Other family
members can ask questions about them and be
encouraging and appreciative about what was shared.

287

*My heart leaps up when I behold a rainbow in the sky
So was it when my life began.*
**WILLIAM WORDSWORTH,
"MY HEART LEAPS UP"**

Take time to look for rainbows and gaze at cloud
formations with your child. Let your hearts leap up
at these miracles of God's creation and be refreshed
by what you see.

288

Every fact in nature is a revelation of God.
GEORGE MACDONALD,
GEORGE MACDONALD: AN ANTHOLOGY

Use objects to demonstrate the truths of God's Word in concrete ways that your children can understand. For example: Using a sponge, you could say: "We need to be like sponges that soak up God's Word and presence (put sponge in water) and are available to be poured or squeezed out to those in the world around us."

289

Comparisons only undermine self-esteem
and foster feelings of inadequacy.
DOROTHY CORKILLE BRIGGS,
"YOUR CHILD'S SELF-ESTEEM"

Refrain from comparing your kids with others (Why can't you make good grades like your brother did?). Instead remind yourself of the ways each of your children is unique and is proceeding on his own and God's timetable.

290

*Goals remain dreams until they are shared
with someone who cares about you.*
**PAULA NELSON,
SOAR WITH YOUR STRENGTHS**

Talk about each family member's goals at the evening
meal and how he or she is going to work toward them.
Sharing goals and hearing encouragement from others
brings accountability into the equation.

291

*I avoid looking forward or backward,
and try to keep looking upward.*
CHARLOTTE BRONTË

Set your sights toward God by meditating
on His Word and spending some time in prayer.
If regrets from the past or concerns about the future
surface in your thoughts, offer them to God and thank
Him for all He has done, all He will do,
and all He is doing.

292

Going to school after a problem arises is like buying the fire engine after the fire has ignited. Be ready before the fire starts; don't wait until it's raging!

PAUL HEATH,
FROM AN INTERVIEW

Develop a relationship with your child's teachers and administrators before a problem occurs. Meet them early in the year; have an individual parent-teacher conference to begin building a working relationship; and show appreciation for the teacher's efforts through notes and treats.

293

Classical music has the potential to challenge and to open new experiences to its listeners that go deep, are lasting, and enrich and educate.

Take your children to symphony concerts and college music department performances and watch them develop a taste for classical music.

294

*Travel provides children tremendous opportunities
to learn history; seeing, hearing, and doing helps children
to understand what would otherwise be distant and abstract.
And travel doesn't have to be to some far away destination.*

Ask your state tourism department for a list
of living history museums and visit them, especially
those in your own backyard. When you do visit a
museum or historical site, discuss what you're seeing
and have your child pick out a postcard and write
about it to grandparents or an out-of-town friend.
When traveling farther away, stop at historical sites
and learn all you can!

295

*It was always important to me that I'm still Lori to my
parents, on or off the [tennis] court. It means a lot that their
love and affection are not based on my winning or losing.
Sometimes parents treat you differently or show
disappointment when your performance is down. . . .
What matters is that their love and support stands.*
LORI MCNEIL, FROM AN INTERVIEW

Let your child know that the process of doing,
participating, and enjoying the sport or activity is
important to you even if she never reaches the top
of her field. Point out the benefits: discipline,
perseverance, self-confidence, and learning how
to work with others, to name a few.

296

We helped our daughters look for their talents and gifts by giving them a wide variety of experiences around our home and, as we could afford it, in the community and through other means: owning pets, 4-H club, camping trips, hobbies, and having friends of all races, ages, and backgrounds.
SALLY CONWAY, FROM AN INTERVIEW

What experiences can you provide around your home and community to stir up your children's interests? List some of these.
▶ Family projects
▶ Hobbies
▶ Community resources
▶ Clubs, Organizations

297

One of the most important aspects of family life is shared meals and conversation. The shared meal is what you might call a family sacrament. If you're going to have this sacrament, it means somebody's got to help mother— kids, husband—somebody has to help cook and clean up, and that should enrich meals because everybody, not just one person, contributes.
ROBERT BELLAH, "HABITS OF THE HEART"

Plan meals for the week and divvy up responsibilities:
▶ Who will set the table?
▶ Who will be the cook's helper?
▶ After everyone takes dishes over to the sink, who has KP duty?

298

A time of recovering from illness can be a close, loving time in which to fill up a child's emotional tank. It can also be profitable in teaching her how to care for someone else who is sick as she observes how she is lovingly cared for.

▶ Write a humorous get-well verse or card each day.
▶ Provide little surprises on the meal tray.
▶ To offset boredom, put a few of your child's favorite activities in a little tote or box by the bed.
▶ Check out lots of library books or books on tape for her to listen to.

299

When an old man dies, a library burns to the ground.
OLD AFRICAN SAYING

Help the elderly people in your family tape-record their oral history with questions you supply. Ask: What is the first house you remember? What was school like? Any war experiences? etc.

300

I have invested much energy showing my three children the importance of being an example of their faith to others. We have relatives who reject our faith in Christ and even ridicule it. Although this is very difficult, we've continued to study God's perspective on this. Jene, my nine-year-old, gave her great-grandma a large-print, red letter Bible for Easter out of her own savings. Great-grandma received it with gratitude.

PEGGY NEWSOME,
FROM AN INTERVIEW

Is there someone in your extended family
that you and your children can share
the love of Christ with this season?

301

Training must come before teaching. Before parents can train their children properly, they must first discipline themselves. An orderly home and orderly habits can be accomplished only by agreeing together on these things.

ELISABETH ELLIOT,
THE SHAPING OF A CHRISTIAN FAMILY

What do you need to be more disciplined about?
What are the areas in which you and your husband
need to be more in agreement? List them, pray about
them, and jot down a plan of action.

302

If we weren't meant to keep starting over,
would God have granted us Monday?

Look forward to Mondays as "new beginning" days.
Here's a sample prayer for a new week: "Lord, I thank
You for the gift of today, this new week, and all You've
planned for me. I give You my life, my eyes, ears, voice,
hands. Use me for Your purpose and Your glory."

303

Children need friends who will affirm and support them.
They also need to see that friendship is like a checking
account and only works if they continue to make deposits.

Teach your child how to be a good friend
both by suggestion ("invite a classmate over"; "when
hurt, forgive your friend quickly"; "be loyal and don't
tell the secrets she shares," etc.) and model
being a good friend.

304

A parent must respect the spiritual person of his child and approach it with reverence, for that too looks the Father in the face and has an audience with Him into which no earthly parent can enter even if he dared to desire it.
GEORGE MACDONALD,
GEORGE MACDONALD: AN ANTHOLOGY

Try asking yourself "How would Christ treat this child?" as you rear your child day by day.

305

God has cast our confessed sins into the depths of the sea, and He's even put a "no fishing" sign over the spot.
DWIGHT L. MOODY

Talk with your child today about the value of confessing sin and the marvelous forgiveness God offers us.

306

*Adjusting and adapting are the keystones
of mother-in-law-hood. These traits make it possible
to play our role well. By thinking the role through,
we can become good mothers-in-law.*
MARY TATEM,
JUST CALL ME MOM

Meditate on 2 Peter 1:5-6 and pick out the
characteristic that will contribute to your success as a
good mother-in-law when your children marry. Look
to changing yourself, not your in-laws; do the most
adjusting as the more mature person, and strive for
godly qualities and communication.

307

*Prayer is a working instrument that does certain things,
like a pencil writes or a knife cuts. Just as you must use
a pencil or knife for it to work, so too you must use prayer
to feel its full power.*
LINDA NEUKRUG,
DAILY GUIDEPOSTS, 1994

Don't miss out on the power, strength,
and wisdom available to you through prayer—
every day! Keep a spiral-bound, index card notebook
on your dresser or kitchen counter with a list of prayer
needs. Ask each family member: "How can I pray for
you this week?" and record their requests in your
prayer journal.

308

Music is . . . a form of remembering,
a return to the seasons of the heart, long ago.
MENOTTI

Share with your children significant music from your
"seasons of the heart": play a rendition of the wedding
march used at your wedding, favorite songs you sang
as a child, hymns, old family favorites.
Pass down a legacy of music!

309

Storytelling has great value for its own sake—
the entertainment and sheer delight a well-told story can
bring to a child. A story is a love-gift from parent to child,
grandparent to grandchild.

You can recover the lost art of spinning a yarn.
Here's how:
► Choose a story you like and read it several times.
► Outline the main events in sequence
(mentally or on paper).
► Try to picture the story in scenes.
► Practice telling the story in your own words
in the mirror.
► Add your own voice inflections, gestures,
props, or musical instrument.

310

*A person lost in his work
has probably found his future.*
RAY RAUCH

Since children tend to be driven by their talents
and abilities during the first ten years of their life,
watch out for their natural inclinations:
► the child who plays a musical instrument by ear;
► the child who draws and paints
and loses track of time;
► the child who takes things apart
or builds elaborate constructions.

311

*Where we love is home—home that our feet may leave,
but not our hearts.*
OLIVER WENDELL HOLMES, SR.

Before your child goes away to college,
make a quilt with forty-nine squares, seven on each
side, that reminds her of the love at home. In the outer
border of squares, friends can write messages with a
laundry marker. The inner squares can show outlined
handprints, messages, and signatures from family
members, grandparents, and other relatives. In the
middle square, stitch your child's name
and the year inside a heart.

312

Parents usually get the behaviors they expect from their children. Why is this? One reason is that children are smart. They sense what the parent expects. They build their own sense of self on the basis of parental expectations. Your child stores these messages in the brain and uses them as ways to measure success or failure, and his own self-worth.

WANDA DRAPER,
YOUR CHILD IS SMARTER THAN YOU THINK

Watch what you say to your child because what you say is what he will mentally record:
PARENT: When will you ever learn?
(CHILD: Maybe I can't learn!)
PARENT: You are more trouble than I can deal with!
(CHILD: I must be a troublemaker.)
PARENT: How many times do I have to tell you?
(CHILD: Is there something wrong with me?)

313

The more you can weave together what your children are learning in the classroom with other subjects—history, art, science—and with real-world activities, the more they will see the big picture of how knowledge interrelates.

Find out from the teacher what units your child is studying in science, history (social studies), literature, and then look for books, videos, and newspaper or magazine articles on those topics and discuss them together.

314

If there were one thing I could change about family trips in my childhood, it would be that instead of just driving by a mountain or forest and seeing it through the car window, I would have experienced it by hiking, touching, and exploring.
KATHY SVEJKOVSKY

On your next trip, don't be too afraid or rushed to get out of the car and take a hands-on approach to traveling. Experiencing and exploring *one or two* places can be more memorable and valuable to a child than rushing by five or six.

315

Our work should not be a distraction from time with Jesus but a reflection.

In all the duties of your day, "practice the presence of God" as Brother Lawrence called it by
► silently lifting your heart up to Him as you work;
► including Him in your conversations by silently praying;
► picturing Him walking by your side;
► offering a quick prayer for the people you pass on the street or in the office or grocery store.

316

Who ran to help me, when I fell,
And would some pretty story tell,
Or kiss the place to make it well?
My mother.
ANN TAYLOR,
"MY MOTHER"

Keep a tote (and a good story) to take out at a moment's notice. In it put Happy Face Band-Aids, ouchless antiseptic, and antibiotic cream. It will save lots of looking when there are scrapes or bike mishaps.

317

Don't equate success with only school-related
or academic pursuits. For some children, especially bodily-
kinesthetic or spatial learners, blooming in life may have
more to do with achieving success in artistic,
mechanical, or athletic areas.
DR. HOWARD GARDNER,
FRAMES OF MIND

Ask your child: What do you like to do most of all? What's fun for you? What are you good at and what do you take pride in? Their answers may carry clues to abilities you hadn't suspected and help you build on their strengths.

318

Children share a characteristic of oatmeal:
When they are heated up, their feelings and thoughts
often bubble to the surface.

Get your child heated up on a regular basis by
engaging him physically: Throw the football
or baseball, play Ping-Pong, or take a brisk walk—
a great stimulator to communication!

319

That energy which makes a child hard to manage
is the energy which afterward makes him a manager of life.
HENRY WARD BEECHER

Think of your most energetic child—the active one
who seems to learn most everything by trial and error.
Thank God for his or her energy and find ways to
channel it in constructive directions: If he can't sit still
as long as the others at the dinner table, he can be the
"waiter" who gets up for things; in the classroom, he
can take notes to the office and pass out papers.

320

A torn jacket is soon mended;
but hard words bruise the heart of a child.
HENRY WADSWORTH LONGFELLOW

Increase the number of loving, positive words to your
child today: "Fantastic job." "You're a joy."
"I knew you could do it."

321

A family vacation is one where you arrive with five bags,
three or four kids, and seven I-thought-you-packed-its!
IVERN BALL,
READER'S DIGEST

To de-stress family travel:
►Have each child make a list of things
he'll need for the trip and pack his own bag.
►Before leaving, pack a tote with activities for on the
road, like Play-Dough, sewing cards, audio cassette
books, postcards to write to a friend, etc.
►Have fun, and if you forgot something, make do!

322

Better a creative mess than tidy idleness.

Are there places for creativity in your house—
for making things, doing puzzles, drawing—
or does everything have to appear perfect? If you have
no place for creativity, make one today.

323

*Music is incredible. Sudden strains of the wedding march . . .
and the whole wedding comes back . . . a few strains
of music, and it all floods back.*
**EDITH SCHAEFFER,
FOREVER MUSIC**

Pick out music to fit the focus and theme of each
holiday and play this music for the whole family.
For example, at Easter, parts of Handel's *Messiah*
or Bach's *St. Matthew's Passion;* at Christmas,
tapes of "Silent Night" and traditional carols.
Near Independence Day, "The Battle Hymn
of the Republic" or "America."

324

Service is the rent we pay for our room on earth.

Whenever any member of the family
does some service or good deed between
Thanksgiving and Christmas, inside or outside
of the family, give him or her a small piece of wool.
Then on Christmas Eve you have a nice amount of
wool which can be braided to put under the cradle of
baby Jesus in the Nativity scene. Year by year the rug
grows and the tradition grows, as do the servant hearts
of you and your children.

325

*Remember that Jesus,
though He stands at the door and knocks
(Revelation 3:20), does not break down the door.*
**DAVID SEAMANDS,
QUOTED IN *PARENTS AND CHILDREN***

When your child closes the door
on communication with you,
►be patient and know this is normal behavior
(especially for young teens);
►continue to express love-in-action;
►verbalize your interest and desire to listen:
"I'm here if you'd like to talk. I'll be glad to listen."

326

*You cannot increase a person's performance
by making him feel worse.*

When your child has failed at a competition
or made a mistake, point out something positive
he did rather than criticize his mistakes. At all cost,
avoid lashing out at him in a negative way
and making him feel worse.

327

*We have always celebrated two birthdays for each of our four
children—their natural birthday and their spiritual birthday.
This has served as a cement in our relationship in reminding
our children that we love them and that their spiritual life is
just as important to us as their birth into our family. In the
teenage years, those two birthdays served as an anchor
to hold them to reality.*

MARY EVANS,
FROM AN INTERVIEW

Decorate the dining room with bright-colored
crepe paper, serve a cake, and have equal numbers
of presents for both birthdays.

328

What would happen if parents told their children,
"Take a stand for what you believe, even if that stand
displeases your teachers or peers,
and know that I will stand behind you"?

JEFF MYERS,
FROM AN INTERVIEW

Talk with your children about qualities
that make a leader. Let them know that bucking the
crowd can be a source of strength and that speaking
up for something you believe in can sometimes
change friends' minds.

329

There are so many adults who quit music lessons as children
and express regrets: "I wish my parents hadn't let me quit."
But I've never heard an adult who regretted
continuing his or her music lessons.

MARILYN ROSFELD,
FROM AN INTERVIEW

Help your child through the "I want to quit" slump by
▸ talking with the teacher and suggesting a change
of music, perhaps to a piece of sheet music;
▸ increasing encouraging words
and decreasing criticism;
▸ giving him reasons to play and share his music—
at church, school, nursing home, etc.;
▸ providing chances to have fun with music—
playing in a duet or improvisational group, composing
a new song on the computer and playing it.

330

Paying children for making certain grades puts undue pressure on them. We find the best students are not paid for grades. Once money has been given, it's harder for the child to experience the process of learning as having been done for its own sake.

DR. ARTHUR BODIN,
FROM AN INTERVIEW

Instead of paying for grades, take your child out
for pizza or a milkshake after a report card or after
meeting personal goals for improvement—just as you
would after a soccer game. It communicates:
"I'm so proud of your hard work!"
It's a celebration, not a payment.

331

The kind word spoken today
may bear its fruit tomorrow.

Write a loving note to your child
with a word of encouragement such as,
"Good luck on your science test!" or "I'm proud
of you and I love you very much." Put it where
he will discover it.

332

*As rewarding as parenthood can be, sometimes
it leaves you feeling swamped, depressed, yearning for an
escape . . . in short, a victim of chronic, unrelieved burnout.*

**CAROL TANNENHAUSER,
"MOTHERHOOD STRESS"**

▸Set priorities so you can do well
the things you really care about.
▸Avoid setting standards so high that you and your
children cannot possibly reach them.
▸Regularly do things that replenish your energy
supplies, and you'll reduce burnout.

333

*Children's lives are our garden. They will remain a garden,
as distinct from a wilderness, only if someone cultivates them.
But they bear witness to God's glory in the very fact that they
need this cultivation, this "weeding and pruning," for like
a garden, they teem with life. And, like a garden, they will
surpass our expectations for them
if they are enabled to do so.*

**MARTI GARLETT,
WHO WILL BE MY TEACHER?**

One of the best ways to cultivate the garden of your
child's life is to recognize learning differences and
patterns and teach in ways that help concepts "click."
If reading the chapter assigned doesn't work, tape-
record it and she can listen to it and follow along. If he
doesn't memorize the multiplication tables as fast as
the other kids, let him practice them orally while
bouncing the basketball.

334

Research showed that when high school students thought their teacher was very motivated and skilled, they performed better than classmates who were not favorably impressed by the teacher's ability.

To help your teen do better in school, start by talking about how outstanding his teachers are. This will raise his expectations for the course and result in higher expectations and standards for himself, which will encourage more effort.

335

You can challenge children without rushing or pressuring them.

Here are some ways to encourage development without pressuring:
▶ Notice what your child can do and arrange activities that are just a little more difficult.
▶ Provide a variety of toys and books that she can play with in her own way.
▶ Remember that you are your child's best teacher!

336

Far away there in the sunshine are my highest aspirations.
I may not reach them, but I can look up and see their beauty,
believe in them, and try to follow where they lead.
LOUISA MAY ALCOTT

Together, read the Charlotte Zolotow book, *Someday*,
and discuss your child's aspirations with him.
Then have him write and illustrate his own *Someday*
book of wishes, dreams, and hopes for the future.

337

A little bit of boredom in your child's life is not the end of the
world. It might lead to her thinking creatively or discovering
a wonderful idea in a new book.

When you child moans, "I'm bored!"
▶ Don't rush to the rescue with a video.
▶ Suggest cleaning out her closet; just the thought
does wonders to stir up creative ideas!
▶ If all else fails, suggest she throw a sheet over a card
table to make a hideaway for reading
and daydreaming.

338

*One of the best ways to help children grow out of
the self-centered stage is to center them on God.*
**GEORGE SELIG AND ALAN ARROYO,
LOVING OUR DIFFERENCES**

Read Bible stories aloud that point to God's character
and highlight people who are living representations of
positive character qualities such as obedience,
trust, and forgiveness.

339

*One of the biggest challenges for parents
is to help our junior high and high school students
develop critical thinking skills and keep an open dialogue
with them about the issues and situations they face, especially
when we disagree with their opinions.
When your child makes a statement contrary to your values:*
► *Instead of overreacting, reason with him.*
► *Help him think it through.*
► *Remember, if we do all their thinking and are so strict
they can't grow, we may drive them away from our home
and from God.*
WENDY FLINT

340

*When schoolchildren from the first through sixth grades
were asked what advice they would most like to give
their parents, the most frequent answer was, "Don't yell."
Yelling does no good, and you can be sure it will
make you feel guilty later.*
PAUL WELTER

If you are on the verge of yelling, go into the bathroom
and wait a moment or two while you meditate on
Matthew 18:21 (which you have taped to the mirror),
"Lord, how many times shall I forgive?"

341

*Neither public, Christian, or home schooling
is any more or less "spiritual." God calls us
to different areas and challenges. And in any situation,
He will use problems to conform us to the image of Christ.*

▶ Visit various school alternatives in your community,
including a home school support meeting.
▶ Talk to parents, teachers, and principals
of each school.
▶ Pray as a family for God's direction
in your choice for your child's education.

342

When our youngest son went off to college . . .
we were unprepared for the ache of parting. When we
parents say, "Someday you'll grow up," we mean a day
in the far-distant future. Not today! The bittersweet
truth is: That day comes much too soon.
MARY JANE CHAMBERS

Do it today—that hug you want to give your child;
that truth you want to convey; the apology you'd like
to make; the chance to say 'I love you.'

343

There is so little empty space. The space is scribbled on;
the time has been filled. . . . Too many activities, and people,
and things. Too many worthy activities, valuable things, and
interesting people. For it is not merely the trivial which
clutters our lives but the important as well.
ANNE MORROW LINDBERGH,
GIFT FROM THE SEA

Take a look at your calendar.
Is there little empty space? Is there any blank space
for just being together, stopping to smell the flowers
in your garden, or sitting by the fire to read?

344

Bitterness and unforgiveness cause us to distance ourselves from people and experiences. When these emotions bubble up, they keep us from participating in and enjoying life.

Today let go of grievances, grudges, and anything that keeps you from loving and being loved.

345

Training the baby by the book is a good idea, only you need a different book for each baby.

Learn about the stages of child development, but don't expect each of your children to develop at the same rate as his or her siblings or your friends' kids. Each child is unique, with a one-of-a-kind brain, gifts, talents, and timetable!

346

Children's brains start immature.
Maturational spurts occur once or twice a year.
It's as if a new computer chip enters in. And when that chip
starts firing, there may be changes in the way
your child learns.

DR. LARRY SILVER, QUOTED IN "LEARNING DISABILITIES:
MASTERING THE CHALLENGE"

If your child doesn't have certain skills today,
keep working with her, supporting her, and believing
in her. When that chip fires, you may see growth,
development, and progress you didn't expect!

347

We make our friends; we make our enemies;
but God makes our next-door neighbor.
G. K. CHESTERTON

Make an effort to meet and get to know
your next-door neighbor. If new neighbors move in,
take over freshly baked bread or a basket of fruit
to welcome them.

348

Silent gratitude isn't very much use to anyone.
ROBERT LOUIS STEVENSON

Who could you thank today?
Your child's school teacher or principal?
Your mailman? Someone who helped you years ago
or just yesterday? Either write and mail the note of
thanks or deliver it orally in person.

349

*We all get hooked into the perfect parent/perfect child myth
and think that child development is a smooth uphill trek with
no obstacles or hurdles. But there are times
that our kids are going to have problems.*
ANN BENJAMIN, FROM AN INTERVIEW

When your children have difficult developmental
times, be there to understand what's underneath the
behavior and to help them through the problem.

350

*The last thing said to a child before a competition,
test, or trial is what he'll remember.*

Right before a violin solo; right before a big exam or
sports competition, make sure that what you say to
your child is positive and will inspire confidence.

351

Children left to grow up like weeds
are not likely to produce the fruits of genius.

Rearing children is not as simplistic as raising flowers
or corn, but there are some analogies.
  ► Have you watered with daily doses
    of encouragement and praise?
  ► Have you weeded out negative influences?
    (Media; too much television?)
  ► Do you add fertilizer (spiritual enrichment,
    reading outside of school)?

352

What a gift a grandparent can be to a young person
unsteady on the path of life.
IRENE M. ENDICOTT, *GRANDPARENTING BY GRACE*

If grandparents are far away, help your child
feel closer to them by making family photo placemats.
Cut poster board to placemat size, glue a yellow circle
in the center, and glue grandparents' and children's
pictures around that. After it dries, cover the placemat
with clear, self-adhesive contact paper, and then use
a rolling pin to press out air bubbles. Allow your
children or teens a weekly long-distance call
to keep in touch with their grandparent.

353

*Music is . . . playing your own tune
while keeping time with the rest of the band.*

Make music together by making rhythm instruments
out of materials around the house: shakers from rice in
a plastic container with tight lid; clackers from two
wooden spoons; drums from a round oatmeal
container. Play music and have your child beat time.
March to the music and have a ball together!

354

*Camping strips away the extras we accumulate,
the busy schedules, the list of chores. It replaces them
with loose schedules, leisurely days, easy interaction,
and beautiful scenery.*
DEBRA BENDIS

For starters, pitch a tent (borrowed, if necessary)
and camp for a weekend. Take easy-to-cook food and
fishing poles if there's a pond or river. Watch the stars
and let your kids store happiness deep inside where
they can find it when they need it most.
Even backyard camping can be memorable.

355

*In the book of Acts, Barnabas was described
as the son of exhortation, which means "encouragement"
or "consolation." When he had witnessed the grace of God
at Antioch, he rejoiced and began to encourage them all
to remain true to the Lord. He stood up for John Mark
when Mark had failed. Most of all, he was willing to be used.*

Are you a Barnabas? If you're willing, you could be
just the person God uses to give someone a pat on the
back, a smile and a cheerful hello, or help someone
in deep trouble.

356

*Time, which changes people,
does not alter the image we have retained of them.*
MARCEL PROUST

When you pick up a package of photos, label your
family's pictures with the event or happening,
the people's names, and the date.

357

*A mother understands
what a child does not say.*
JEWISH PROVERB

What is your child trying to say today in actions,
attitudes, and expressions that he or she cannot say
in words? Be sensitive to these nonverbal means
of expression and pray for an understanding heart.

358

*A hug can soothe a small child's pain
and bring a rainbow after rain.
The hug! There's just no doubt about it. . . .
A hug delights and warms and charms,
it must be why God gave us arms.*

Stretch out your arms today
and give someone a hug or two, especially
your husband and children! Research shows
every person needs at least four hugs a day.

359

*How many there are who fail to realize
that the measure of gifts lies not in their size or splendor
but in the spirit of their giving!*
**DORTHEA S. KOPPLIN,
SOMETHING TO LIVE BY**

Before dinner today, ask each person in the family
to write a redeemable coupon for a service they will
give to another family member. Put each coupon
in an envelope and set it beside the appropriate
family member's plate.

360

*Let the children laugh and be glad.
O my dear, they haven't long before the world assaults them.
Allow them a genuine laughter now. Laugh with them,
till tears run down your faces—till a memory of pure delight
and precious relationship is established within them,
indestructible, personal, and forever.*
WALTER WANGERIN

Don't be a killjoy. When your children laugh,
relax and laugh with them!

361

Life, misfortunes, isolation, abandonment, poverty,
are battlefields which have their heroes; obscure heroes,
sometimes greater than the illustrious heroes.
VICTOR HUGO

Ask your children to identify an outstanding
Christian. Have them write down the person's name
and discuss why they see him or her as a committed,
sincere Christian.

362

Tell me my story
Let me see
The laughing tiny baby that
I used to be.
Tell me why I'm special and of
The love you have for me.
CAROL OTIS HURST

Get out your child's baby pictures and tell him some
stories that happened in his first few months of life;
how special the birth and delivery were; how thrilled
you were to welcome him into the family.

363

*Children and teenagers need us at the most unpredictable
and often most inconvenient times—sometimes right after
school or at midnight after a date. This is when they open up
and talk about their thoughts, feelings, hurts, and dreams.
These are "prime times" for parents. Don't miss them!*

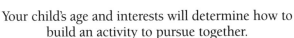

Whatever your child's prime times for communication,
determine to be there—available, listening,
and caring.

364

*A key to developing a relationship with your child
is to find something to do together that you both enjoy.*

Your child's age and interests will determine how to
build an activity to pursue together.
Here are some ideas:
▶ Read the same paperback book he is assigned
for school and talk it over.
▶ If he or she is into sports, throw or kick the ball,
hit golf balls at the driving range, or . . . ?
▶ Bike together; plan outings to museums.
▶ Look for earrings and treasures
at thrift and vintage shops.

365

*Jesus said, "Let the little children come to me,
and do not hinder them, for the kingdom of heaven
belongs to such as these."*
MATTHEW 19:14 (NIV)

Take your children to church;
don't just drop them off, go together.
Sit together in church
until they reach the point where they need
to be with their peers.

EPILOGUE

I'd like to leave you with this little prayer I found during a challenging time of my life when we were living in Maine:

> Lord,
> Thank You for upheaval,
> for rocking my little boat.
> For sending winds that seem too strong and
> Waves that threaten to capsize me,
> Because all of this drives me into Your arms,
> And anything which
> results in that end,
> Lord,
> is worth getting
> wet over.

The next time life seems to rock your boat and bring upheaval and difficulty your way, I pray that you'll let it drive you into the arms of your heavenly Father, and you'll find rest in His everlasting, always-available love for *you*, and the strength and wisdom that you need as a mother.

✤   ✤   ✤

I'd love to hear from you if you'd like to share *your* favorite mothering tip, humorous story, or a quote that's inspired you. Jot it down and write to me at Yellow Roses and Encouraging Words, P.O. Box 770493, Oklahoma City, OK 73177.

BIBLIOGRAPHY

Abrams, M. H., ed. *The Norton Anthology of English Literature*. New York: W.W. Norton & Company, 1987.

Anglund, Joan Walsh. *The Circle of the Spirit*. New York: Random House, 1983.

Baldwin, Bruce A. *It's All in Your Head*. Wilmington, NC: Direction Dynamics, 1985.

Barnes, Emilie. *The Spirit of Loveliness*. Eugene, OR: Harvest House Publishers, 1994.

Billheimer, Paul. *Don't Waste Your Sorrows*. Fort Washington, PA: Christian Literature Crusade, 1977.

Bonhoeffer, Dietrich. *Life Together*. New York: Harper-Collins, 1982.

Bradstreet, Anne. *The Works of Anne Bradstreet*. Jeannine Hensley, ed. Cambridge, MA: The Belknap Press of Harvard University Press, 1967.

Briggs, Dorothy Corkille. *Your Child's Self-Esteem*. New York: Doubleday, 1975.

Buckley, Gail Lumet. *The Hornes: An American Family*. New York: New American Library, Penguin, 1988.

Campbell, Ross. *How to Really Love Your Teenager*. Wheaton: Victor Books, 1986.

Carmichael, Amy. *If*. Fort Washington, PA: Christian Literature Crusade, 1938.

Carson, Ben. *Gifted Hands*. Grand Rapids, MI: Zondervan Books, 1990.

Cather, Willa. *O Pioneers!* New York: Houlton, 1913.

Chervin, Ronda. *Prayer Exercises for Mothers*. Pecos, NM: Dove Publications, 1980.

Daily Guideposts, 1994. Carmel, NY: GUIDEPOSTS, 1994.

Dobson, James. *Parenting Isn't For Cowards*. Dallas: Word Publishing, 1987.

Draper, Wanda. *Your Child Is Smarter Than You Think*. Oklahoma City: Omni Family Productions, 1993.

Drescher, John. *If I Were Starting My Family Again*. Intercourse, PA: Good Books, 1994.

Drescher, John. *Seven Things Children Need*. Scottsdale, AZ: Herald Press, 1976.

Dunn, David. *Try Giving Yourself Away*. Englewood Cliffs, NJ: Prentice Hall, Inc., 1956.

Elkind, David. *The Hurried Child*. Reading, MA: Addison-Wesley Publishing Company, 1981.

Elliot, Elisabeth. *Let Me Be a Woman*. Wheaton, IL: Tyndale, 1976.

Elliot, Elisabeth. *The Shaping of a Christian Family*. Nashville, TN: Thomas Nelson Publishers, 1992.

Endicott, Irene M. *Grandparenting by Grace: A Guide Through the Joys and Struggles*. Nashville: Broadman & Holman, 1994.

Farmer, Richard Allen. *It Won't Fly If You Won't Try: How to Let Your Creative Genius Take Flight*. Portland, OR: Multnomah, 1992.

Fleming, Jean. *A Mother's Heart*. Colorado Springs, CO: NavPress, 1982.

Frank, Anne. *The Diary of a Young Girl*. New York: Doubleday, 1974.

Fuller, Cheri. *HOME-LIFE: The Key to Your Child's Success at School.* Tulsa, OK: Honor Books: 1988.

Fuller, Cheri. *How to Grow a Young Music Lover: Helping Your Child Discover and Enjoy the World of Music.* Wheaton, IL: Harold Shaw Publishers, 1994.

Fuller, Cheri. *Motivating Your Kids from Crayons to Career.* Tulsa, OK: Honor Books, 1990.

Fuller, Cheri. *Unlocking Your Child's Learning Potential.* Colorado Springs, CO: Piñon Press, 1994.

Fuller, Cheri. *Helping Your Child Succeed in Public School.* Colorado Springs, CO: Focus on the Family, 1993.

Fuller, Cheri. *Creating Christmas Memories: Family Traditions for a Lifetime.* Tulsa, OK: Honor Books, 1991.

Gardner, Howard. *Frames of Mind: The Theory of Multiple Intelligences.* New York: Basic Books, Inc., 1993.

Garlett, Marti. *Who Will Be My Teacher?* Waco, TX: Word Books, 1985.

George, Alice N., ed. *The Complete Poetical Works of Wordsworth.* Cambridge, MA: The Riverside Press, 1932.

Glenn, H. Stephen. *Raising Self-Reliant Children in a Self-Indulgent World.* Rocklin, CA: Prima Publishing, 1989.

Graham, Ruth Bell. *It's My Turn.* Old Tappan, NJ: Revell, 1982.

Graham, Ruth Bell. *Prodigals and Those Who Love Them.* Colorado Springs, CO: Focus on the Family Publishing, 1991.

Hession, Roy. *The Calvary Road*. Fort Washington, PA: Christian Literature Crusade, 1950.

Holmes, Marjorie. *I've Got to Talk to Somebody, God*. Garden City, NY: Doubleday, 1968.

Holmes, Marjorie. *To Help You Through the Hurting*. Garden City, NY: Doubleday, 1983.

Hunt, Mary. *The Best of The Cheapskate Monthly*. New York: St. Martin's Press, 1993.

Hunt, Gladys. *Honey for a Child's Heart*. Grand Rapids, MI: Zondervan, 1969.

Keller, Helen. *The Story of My Life*. New York: Avon Books, 1990.

Kesler, Jay; Ron Beers; LaVonne Neff. *Parents and Children*. Wheaton, IL: Victor Books, 1987.

Kopplin, Dorothea S. *Something to Live By*. Garden City, NY: Garden City Books, 1945.

L'Engle, Madeleine. *Walking on Water: Reflections on Faith and Art*. Wheaton, IL: Harold Shaw Publishers, 1980.

Laubach, Frank. *Christ Liveth in Me* and *Game With Minutes*. Westwood, NJ: Fleming Revell, 1946.

Lehmkuhl, Dorothy; Dolores Cotter Lamping. *Organizing for the Creative Person*. New York: Crown Publishers, 1993.

Lewis, C.S., ed. *George MacDonald: An Anthology*. New York: Macmillan, 1974.

Lindbergh, Anne Morrow. *Gift From the Sea*. New York: Phoenix Press, 1984.

Linscott, Robert N., ed. *Selected Poems & Letters of Emily Dickinson*. New York: Doubleday, 1959.

Marshall, Catherine. *Adventures in Prayer*. New York: Ballantine Books, 1975.

McBridge, Angela Barron. *The Secret of a Good Life with Your Teenager*. New York: Times Books, 1987.

Menconi, Al; Dave Hart. *Today's Music: A Window to Your Child's Soul*. Elgin, IL: David C. Cook, 1990.

Moyers, Bill. *A World of Ideas*. New York: Doubleday, 1990.

Nelson, James D. *Uncommon Friends*. New York: Harcourt Brace Jovanovich, 1987.

Nelson, Paula; Donald O. Clifton. *Soar with Your Strengths*. New York: Delacorte Press, 1992.

Oke, Janette. *Father of Love*. Minneapolis, MN: Bethany, 1989.

Peck, M. Scott. *The Road Less Travelled*. San Franscisco: Touchstone Books, 1980.

Reardon, Ruth. *Listen to the Littlest*. Norwalk, CT: C. R. Gibson, 1984.

Schaeffer, Edith. *What Is a Family?* Old Tappan, NJ: Fleming H. Revell Company, 1975.

Schaeffer, Edith. *Forever Music: A Tribute to the Gift of Creativity*. Grand Rapids, MI: Baker Book House, 1986.

Selig, George; Alan Arroyo. *Loving Our Differences*. Virginia Beach, VA: CBN Publishing, 1989.

Shakespeare, William. *Hamlet*. New York: Simon & Schuster, 1975.

Smith, Hannah Whitall. *God Is Enough*. New York: Ballantine Books, 1986.

Tatem, Mary. *Just Call Me Mom.* Camp Hill, PA: Christian Publications, 1994.

Thoene, Bodie. *Munich Signature.* Minneapolis, MN: Bethany House, 1990.

Wangerin, Walter. *Ragman and Other Cries of Faith.* New York: Harper-Collins, 1984.

Warren, Rick. "Fax of Life." Mission Viejo, CA: self-published, 1994.

Welty, Eudora. *One Writer's Beginnings.* New York: Warner Books, 1983.

Werner, Hazen G. *Christian Family Living.* Nashville: The Graded Press, 1958.

Whitehead, John. *The Stealing of America.* Wheaton, IL: Crossway Books, 1983.

Wilson, Mimi; Mary Beth Lagerborg. *Once a Month Cooking.* Colorado Springs, CO: Focus on the Family Publishing, 1992.

Woods, Margolyn. *Grandma's Little Activity Book.* Tulsa, OK: Honor Books, 1994.

Yates, Elizabeth. *A Book of Hours.* New York: Walker, 1985.

Yorkey, Mike. *Growing A Healthy Marriage.* Colorado Springs, CO: Focus on the Family Publishing, 1993.

NOTES

1. Reported in "Fussy Baby Blues," *Christian Home & School* magazine (April 1989), page 9.

2. Finley Eversole, *The Politics of Creativity*, quoted in Madeleine L'Engle's *Walking on Water: Reflections on Faith and Art* (Wheaton, IL: Harold Shaw Publishers, 1980), page 72.

3. Dorothea S. Kopplin, *Something to Live By* (Garden City, NY: Garden City Books, 1945), page 117.

4. Jean Lush on Focus on the Family broadcast "Women and Stress," February 8-9, 1993.

5. Rick Warren, "Fax of Life," July 25, 1994, self-published.

6. Mary Hunt, *The Best of the Cheapskate Monthly*, pages 67-74.

7. Warren, "Fax of Life," July 18, 1994.

8. University of Kansas Study, reported in "Focus on the Family Bulletin," Carol Stream, IL: Tyndale House Publishers (January 1989).

9. "Waiting," United Press Syndicate, n.d.

10. *What Works: Research About Teaching and Learning*, United States Department of Education, 1986.

11. See my book *How to Grow a Young Music Lover* for a variety of resources, including tapes, CD's, videos, and more.